TOMORROW NEVER LIES

Life is about the choices we make.

Your life today is about the choices made yesterday.

Your life tomorrow will be about the choices
you make today.

Choose carefully.

Because tomorrow never lies.

i

TOMORROW NEVER LIES

Written by

Ken Gordon

with

Rachel Orr

Published by

TNL Enterprises Inc.

Canadian Cataloguing in Publication Data
ISBN: 0-9698622-1-0
Gordon, Ken with Rachel Orr, 2000-
Tomorrow Never Lies

Printed & bound in Canada.
First Printing - October 2000

Stories and characters are drawn from the experiences and perceptions of the authors. Personal names and event details are fictitious. Quotes gratefully acknowledged from "Quote Me", compiled by J. Edward Breslin.

This book is dedicated to
anyone who will dare to dream,
and sustain the courage
to pursue that dream
with passion.

Acknowledgements

I am truly grateful to Rachel Orr for her enormous and endless effort and commitment in co-writing Tomorrow Never Lies. Her awesome talent as a writer, and her creativity have taken the book to a higher level of practicality and value for the reader. Working with her over the last 10 months was a very enjoyable and rewarding experience. We worked so well as a team because we were firm believers in the end result. Thanks for being a great partner.

To my great friend Alex Graffos. It is so awesome to have someone like you in my life to share each other's dreams and goals. Thank you.

Thanks to my wife Shawna and our three children, Cody, Chase and Montana for giving me a wonderfully balanced life and for reminding me every single day how precious life is.

And finally, to you Mom. I know you're up there watching over us. I also know this book would make you feel so very proud. Well, Ruthie, this one, most definitely, is for you.

— Ken Gordon

For those who dare to dream. . .

The greatest achievements come from independent vision—individuals, families who have the ability to separate fact from fiction and have the drive and intrinsic motivation to take real action. They don't accept the status quo. They have their lives and theirs families at the forefront of their life plan. They don't run from a challenge, they embrace it. They use common sense and patience to get through periods of uncertainty. They are conservative but still believe they can have it all.

They have the ability to make objective decisions and don't feel compelled to follow the latest and greatest trend. They run their personal and family money management like a successful Fortune 500 company. They have undeniable focus on adding value to the shareholders — their family. When viewed in that context, it's never just another day at the office.

Ask yourself. . . if the future came tomorrow, would you be ready? By living each day and making decisons based on your dreams for the future, you truly can have the life you've imagined. Tomorrow never lies. So whatever stage you and your family are at, Tomorrow Never Lies can work for you. As Abraham Lincoln said "The best thing about the future is that it only comes one day at a time."

— Ken Gordon

Table of Contents

"We are not what we think we are,
but what we think, we are."
—Anonymous

Introduction

Life is about choices.

Of there is any one thing that accounts for our universal rise in stress levels, it may be the astounding myriad of choices we all face and make. Every single day.

In fact, life can come at us so fast that we are barely aware of the relentless selection process. We are involved in this process, whether we like it or not, simply by showing up for life each day. As a coping strategy, many of us learn to make our choices with barely a thought given.

A classic example of this is driving. Every day we travel to and from work and arrive safely at our destination without really thinking about it. We may have changed lanes a dozen times, swerved to prevent an accident, stopped at all the red lights and even zipped down a shortcut we know to use when traffic in a certain area is backed up. We can do all of this every day without really thinking about it. Our routes are so familiar and we've driven for so many years that it has all become a habit.

We routinely engage or prevent certain activities without having to think and consciously examine our alternatives before we decide on an appropriate course of action. This is called habitual behavior, and as illustrated by the driving example above, it can be a successful coping strategy.

It can also be a very dangerous thing.

Some life choices require serious deliberation before committing them to action or habit. And sometimes, especially if pertinent factors of the equation have changed, we may need to remake our decisions. Some choices can work well for us for years. But if things can change — and we can all agree that change is a given in the current equation of life — these same choices that once helped us get what we want stop working. If this happens, and we neglect to notice and make the necessary adjustments, the results can be catastrophic.

This is easily noticed in the business world. Companies try to monitor changes in their marketplace. They know it is important to react in time, and reinvent themselves when necessary in order to remain successful. Without a solid strategy and course of action to compensate for changes in the marketplace as and when they occur, any business is almost certain to fail.

It was during a conversation with a colleague one morning that it occurred to me just how many similarities there are between a successful business and a successful family. The more we explored the concept, the more we realized how the positive strategies of a successful corporation could be overlaid on the family unit.

In many ways, this book is the result of that conversation.

My objective is to share with you some priceless bits of wisdom I've picked up along the way that have enriched my life as well as the lives of others. And I do mean enriched — this book is about money. It is also about life — dreams, goals, plans and how to achieve them.

If there's one thing my work and my clients have taught me, it is that you can't talk about money without talking about life's components: desires, goals, realities, restrictions, and that unpredictable thing called chance. Our lives are about the choices we make.

In many ways, my life may be similar to yours. My wife and I struggle and marvel at the challenges and rewards of raising a family. We ponder the future for our children and wonder what life will be like for them when they are our age. We want them to do well and be well. We believe one way to help ensure this is to do well, and be well ourselves. We trust in the likelihood that children learn from our example. If life is about the choices we make, we want to make sure our children know this.

So What is Choice?

I like to define choice as a decision followed by related and sustained action. Making a choice requires a decision, and must be followed by action. Without the action, a choice has not been made. Except maybe the unconscious choice to lose by default, because that is often what happens when we do not take action.

With each decision we make, we technically make quite a few others simply as a result of the original decision. When you choose to go to Maui for your vacation, you choose not to go to Italy, Florida or Spain. Or any other place, for that matter. Every choice has consequence.

Sometimes people tell me they can't make a choice; they don't know what they want. These folks seem to know only what they don't want. It's a start, maybe, but from where I sit, life could get excessively complicated if all our choices are made based on what we don't want.

Let's say you are out for dinner and the dessert trolley has arrived at your table. Here are your options:

1. Let your eyes rove over the selection and pick the most appealing.

2. Wait to see what others select, and take what they choose.

3. Wait to see what others select and then take something totally different.

4. Reach for the fresh fruit because you know you reached your caloric count already with dinner.

5. Go for your heart's desire because when you ordered your dinner, you saved some calories for dessert.

6. Skip dessert altogether.

Is any choice more right than another? No. And that's the point I want to make regarding decisions and choices. We all make our own, based on our own rules (or lack of them).

And we live with the consequences of our choices.

People hopelessly unable to make a choice will lose by default. Because they can't decide, and act on that decision, they will never really be in the game. Either all the desserts will be eaten, have gone stale, or the restaurant will close and you will be asked to leave. With indecision, nobody wins.

This book is about growing real wealth — in the real world. If I had to put it in as few words as possible as to what this book is about, I would describe it as how to grow wealth — real wealth — *in the real world.* The real world is my world. It is the only one I care to know. And real wealth is about more than just having money, as the following little story illustrates so well.

> One day a father and his rich family took his son on a trip to the country with the firm purpose of showing him how poor people can be. They spent a day and a night at the farm of a very poor family. When they returned from their trip, the father asked his son, "How was the trip?"
>
> "Very good, Dad!"
>
> "Did you see how poor people can be?" the father asked.
>
> "Yeah!"

"And what did you learn?"

The son replied: "I saw that we have a dog at home and they have four. We have a pool that reaches to the middle of the garden; they have a creek that has no end. We have imported lamps in the garden; they have the stars. Our patio reaches to the front yard; they have a whole horizon."

When the little boy finished speaking, his father was speechless. His son added, "Thanks, Dad, for showing me how poor we are."

I have learned that real wealth is more than money. It involves attitudes, action and purpose. I'm going to shoot straight from the hip, so to speak, and tell it to you like I see it. I will do this because I want to make a difference in your life. I can't do that very well if I water things down, or hold back. But in the end, the ball will be in your court.

You must be the one to make the decisions that are right for you. And you are the one that must act on them. I hope you do. As radio and television personality Bill Good has said —

*"More has been lost to procrastination
than to wrong decisions."*
—Bill Good

Introduction Review

- Life is about choices.

- In the course of our life, we may be wise to remake some of our choices.

- A choice is a decision followed by related and sustained action.

- In the game of life, we can lose by default if we fail to make our own choices.

- Real wealth is about more than just having money.

Chapter One

~

You Can't Go Through Life on a Hockey Stick.

Chapter One

~

You Can't Go Through Life on a Hockey Stick.

I will always remember my fifth grade teacher, and certain words she unceremoniously spoke one day. But before I tell you what they were, I must set the stage for you . . .

The year was 1969. Among the group of boisterous young fellows in the class there was one that always stood out. It wasn't because he was the noisiest or most raucous, although his energy levels could have easily won him either position.

It wasn't because he was the most scholarly. His older brother and sister competed for this honor. In fact, while his older brother was being bestowed the distinction of "Most Likely to Succeed" at graduation, the school principal took the opportunity to wisecrack that the younger brother was the strongest candidate for "Most UNlikely to Succeed".

This young boy was judged to be different from the rest by just about everybody. It was as if he bore an undeniable physical deformity. Classmates, parents, teachers and even total strangers all shared the same opinion. He was constantly singled out for one reason: he was short. Really, really short.

Despite his diminutive stature, he was a zealous athlete. Even though his team mates towered over him, he made up for his lack of size with passion and commitment. So much so, that he earned a position on the basketball and hockey teams. He played hard for every game, and he was especially enthusiastic about hockey. As did many boys his age, he dreamed of being the next Bobby Orr. He never, ever wore socks in his skates after he learned that Bobby Orr never wore socks. Hockey was always on his mind. He constantly doodled goalies in the margins of his books and on scraps of paper everywhere.

The academic side of school, however, took second place in this young fellow's mind. He struggled with his studies and was often reminded by both his parents and his teachers that his intellect was decidedly inferior to his siblings'. However, one teacher in particular, took it upon herself to highlight the importance of an education.

"You can't go through life on a hockey stick," she wailed.

This was pretty brutal information to my eleven year old self. (Yes, I was the young fellow being described.) It took a few years for me to get my head around her message.

While I could still, to this day, question their timing and delivery, it is impossible to deny the impact those words had on me in ways that I'm sure were not intended. By the time I'd finished my teen years, I knew I had to find something suitable, and productive to do with my life. I could not follow in the family footsteps to university on scholarships — they said I wasn't smart enough.

Coming out from underneath the stigma of intellectual inferiority was a key element to finding my own way. It happened the year I enrolled in college and studied two subjects: business law and marketing. These subjects inspired me, and to everyone's amazement, including my own, I rose to the top of the class. I have never looked back. It is amazing what happens when you find the right niche for yourself.

Dare to Dream

One of the best things I did as a little kid was to dream. With the natural naivete afforded my tender age, I would imagine my future as the next living hockey legend. I did so frequently, and with a detailed and vivid imagination. I could hear the crowd roar with every game-winning goal. I could feel the boards as I fought in the corners and won the puck every time. Let me tell you, winning felt wonderful! I studied every move of my hero Bobby Orr, and did my utmost to emulate him every time I laced up my skates.

It never occurred to me that I was dreaming an impossible dream. That is, until Ms. Burst-my-Bubble delivered her reality check in the fifth grade with her proclamation that I wouldn't be able to go through life on a hockey stick. I soon found there were others who agreed with her. They cited my lack of size and the indisputable fact that of those who try, very few make it in professional hockey as reasons why I should give up on my dream. How do you argue with other people's reality when you are eleven years old?

Today I know I would ask, "What about Yvan Cournoyer? Paul Kariya? Or Cliff Ronning or Theo Fleury?"

I would point out that despite their small physical size, they are all doing quite nicely going through life on a hockey stick. For that matter, I would point out that pint-sized John Stockton is also going through life quite nicely with a basketball as his vehicle of choice. There are numerous examples of undersized athletes with oversized performances and salaries to match. Certainly enough to adequately challenge any theory regarding size. Of the seven biggest NBA players, not one played in the 1999 All-Star Game. Truth is, taller isn't necessarily better in the National Basketball Association. Or anywhere else, for that matter. Unless you are a ladder.

"Yesterday is but today's memory,
and tomorrow is today's dream."
—Anonymous

It is not that I sit around and wonder what would have happened if I had pursued a hockey career. I don't. Not for a minute. However, as a parent now, I would never discourage my son from doing anything simply because he is smaller than others. Or because only a few make it to the top. I have since learned that making choices for oneself are best not based on what other people think or believe.

Nonetheless, I relinquished my dream of becoming a professional hockey player by the time I graduated from high school. I did not know what I was going to do with the rest of my life; I just knew it wasn't going to be hockey.

But I came away from high school with something very valuable. Something that wasn't even taught then. Through my boyhood imaginings of hockey stardom — *I had learned how to dream!*

To my knowledge, this still isn't taught in school, and I think that's sad. As a child, I knew what it felt like to visualize myself "reaching the stars," and it felt good. I knew what it felt like to have a goal and be actively engaged in activities that would help me reach it. That felt good, too.

It wasn't until years later that I came to realize how well those skills I practiced as a child would serve me. The ability to dream with courage and a vivid imagination are foundational to my life. The ability to dream with skill is a valuable skill.

It is a skill I have honed and one I hope to teach you in this book. For now, suffice it to say that dreams are vital. Dreams are where it all begins. Not much happens without them.

It is not impossible that life can toss a windfall our way and hand it to us on a silver platter. But the odds are dismally low. Most times, if you listen carefully to someone who has achieved success, you will often hear snippets about childhood dreams that came true — in between the words about hard work, effort and persistence.

It Takes Courage to Dream

It takes courage and bravery to dream. I admire anyone who has the courage. Anyone who has never done it can't begin to appreciate how *much* courage it takes. I'm not talking about daydreaming. Daydreaming is that enjoyable but mindless meandering and musing. That is fantasizing, and it's not what I mean when I say dreaming.

Dreaming means "sticking your neck out," if only to yourself, and declaring your intentions. Expressing something you want to be, do or have. Once you have done that, you have made a type of commitment to yourself. After that, if you don't pursue the dream, part of you will always know this. You will always know you did not honor your commitment to yourself by even trying to achieve the dream. Those are not the seeds for happiness.

And if you have been brave enough to declare the dream in front of others, and not just to yourself, you have really done it. You have laid yourself on the line and set yourself up to be reminded by those who heard you. They might not let you forget it. Some people have very long memories and will remind you at the most inopportune of times. There's no question about it: you risk when you verbalize a dream.

It is much easier, and safer, to take a "wait-and-see-what-happens" approach. That way, no matter what happens to us in life, we can feel immune from responsibility. We never said what we were setting out to do, so no one will ever know if we achieved it or not. No one can label us as a failure, or a loser.

Or so we might think.

We might think so, but it would be faulty thinking. Not dreaming is a way of not really participating in your own life. Sure, we might not come off as a loser, but we'll never come off as a winner, either. Not to anyone, and especially not to ourselves.

How can we? We were never really in the game.

Dream at Any Age

Many people whom we admire as successful in their field acknowledge childhood roots to their goals. Jay Leno, arguably the most successful nighttime talk show host since Johnny Carson, can describe in detail when he made his dream to become a stand-up comic.

Jay Leno was twelve, and attending a ceremony where his dad, an insurance salesman, was being presented with an award. During the acceptance speech his dad gave, he cracked a couple of jokes and made everyone laugh. Jay says he watched in amazement at the audience and remembers thinking that his dad was the most powerful person in the room. He marveled at his dad's power to make people laugh. He says it was at that moment he was hooked, and he knew his dream was to become a stand-up comic.

From sport stars, to movie idols to the great inventors of this world, many affirm their ultimate arrival at success began with a dream. They were all different dreams, but they all had dreams.

Actor Jim Carrey claims to have carried a certain check in his wallet for years before he was paid millions to make movies. He had made the check himself, payable to himself, in the amount of the millions he eventually was paid. He kept it in his wallet to constantly remind himself of his dream. That is called having a dream you believe in!

Magic Johnson's dreams were on the basketball court. Albert Einstein's spanned the entire universe as his mind took his dreams to places no one had ever been. Walt Disney's were about an entertainment park. Mother Teresa's were of a kind, caring and loving world. The variety of dreams is endless and not all are formed in youth. Colonel Sanders was over 60 years of age and retired before he made his dream a fast food success story.

And then there is Bill Gates. Imagine the dreams he must have! You can be sure of a couple of things here. One, you can be sure Billy Gates has dreams. Big ones. Two, you can be absolutely certain that they are no more important than yours.

Different People, Different Dreams

Not all dreams or life goals are about fame and fortune. I've known people whose dream has very little to do with money. They simply want to be the very best they can become at their occupation. They wish to be the best school teacher, the best cabinetmaker, the best retailer or the best at whatever it is they do. Their pride in their work is the fuel that keeps them going.

Some people want a peaceful life filled with a loving family. For them, being at something like a family picnic where they are surrounded by the entire immediate family and their offspring is nothing short of nirvana. Their family is everything and everything is their family.

For other people, the creation of a horticultural paradise in their backyard is the ultimate accomplishment. Different noble souls in the field of medicine toil away in their labs harboring a dream to discover a much needed cure. Others gravitate to more athletic aspirations — they want to pitch the perfect game, or make a hole-in-one, or break a record.

Different people have different dreams. That's the way it should be. There is no right or wrong dream. What is right for someone is right . . . *for them*. It is not necessarily right for someone else. What is right for you is right for you.

Dreams require no justification. We are all motivated by different forces. We hear different drummers, and it is important that we listen for our own.

Sometimes there is no mistaking their origin and reason, such as when dreams are motivated by life-changing events. Christopher Reeves, at the time of the writing of this book, is still dreaming about the day he will walk again. He won't listen to anyone who tries to talk him out of it, or tell him it is impossible. He is fixed on his dream. It is what keeps him going. It is a driving force, as can be any dream.

It doesn't matter *what* your dream is. It only matters greatly that you *have* one. Sadly, many of us have lost touch with our dreams, although at some point in our lives we have had them. But it is never too late to get them back, or make a new one.

So... what is your Dream?

Life is about the choices we make, and no choice we make is as important as the one that determines which dream we will pursue. I'm not talking about short term dreams here, like where you're going to spend your next vacation. I'm talking about The Big Picture. Your Life Dream.

In your mind, what does life hold for you (and your spouse if you have one) at the end of the rainbow in your retirement years? What are your plans? How do you see your life, when all is said and done? More importantly, how are you going to get there? How will you live you life along the way?

If you are like most people reading this book, you will not be able to answer those questions. At least not easily. Few people have a plan for their life. But not having a plan is like losing by default, and it can have serious consequences.

Would you ever embark on a trip in unfamiliar territory without a map, directions or knowing the location of your destination? Of course not! You wouldn't know which direction to head first. If anyone suggested that you go off on such a trip without appropriate plans and preparation, you would think them crazy.

Well, from where I sit, living without a Life Plan is equally crazy. Yet so many people do it.

We will spend countless hours planning our vacation in all its details. In great specifics, we plan when we'll go, how we'll get there, what we will wear, what we will do and the people we will do it with. Even if it's just a weekend camping trip!

Yet when it comes to our Life Plans, the pages are often blank.

We agonize for countless hours over which college or university is best for our children. And we're good at it! By the time they are of the age that college is an issue, we've already had years of practice with the public versus private school debate.

As a species, we are very capable of making plans and choices. It is how we have survived. Without an ability to plan for the seasons when food would be scarce, such as winter, as a race we would not have survived. We have thousands of years of experience at planning and choosing.

Real estate agents assure me their clients spend vast amounts of time finding and choosing homes. If we don't know what we want when we start looking at houses, we soon figure it out. Sometimes we start with defining what we don't want before we can define what we *do* want. Whatever our methodology, sooner or later we arrive at a decision. We select our home and plan the move.

But that's not the end of the planning and choosing. Some people will then devote hours upon many more hours pouring over Martha Stewart magazines in order to carefully plan their decor.

Think about your last vehicle purchase. How many hours did you spend researching, planning and deciding? If you add up the time you spent on the internet checking things out, and the time spent admiring the contenders in magazine ads, talking about it, reading automobile reviews

21

and generally researching your options, it would probably total quite a few hours. Yet in the overall scheme of life, how much difference will it make as to what car we drive? How important is that decision compared with one that determines how you will spend the rest of your life?

I'm not suggesting that the next time you buy a new car that you should make your choice by throwing darts at the classified ads section of the newspaper. It is always wise to do your research and buy wisely.

However, I am suggesting that you spend an equally proportionate amount of time making and preserving your dreams. Many people spend more time figuring out what they are going to wear to a Christmas party than they do making decisions about their future.

I say be different. Dream your dreams, whatever they may be. And take actions according to your own, self-designed Life Plan based on that dream. If you haven't already got one, keep reading this book and I'll help you get it. What's more, I'll teach you some techniques that will greatly improve the odds that you'll achieve it.

Don't think it's easy. It isn't.

Is it worth it? You bet it is! In fact, it is worth everything, and more, that you put into it.

"There is no medicine like hope, no incentive so great, and no tonic so powerful as expectation of something better tomorrow."
—Orison Swett Marden

Chapter One Review

- Yesterday is today's memory, and tomorrow is today's dream.

- It's best not to make our choices based on what other people think, feel, believe or want. Our choices must be our own.

- The ability to dream with skill is valuable.

- It takes courage to dream.

- We can make a dream at any age.

- There are no right or wrong dreams. Different people have different dreams.

- No one's dream is more important than ours.

- Living without a dream and a Life Plan is crazy.

- We only have one life.

Chapter Two

Different Choices
Different Lives

Chapter Two

Different Choices
Different Lives

"It's an immutable law of nature that each generation will dress, speak, make love and listen to music in the way best calculated to infuriate their elders."
—Anonymous

What we choose to believe, as well as other life choices we make, seem to have an interesting link to our attitudes. I don't know which comes first, the attitudes or the choices, but each generation is somewhat different.

Each generation has its own music, political agenda, style preferences and social habits. Each experiments with different ways to raise and educate their children. Each generation seems to have its own unique set of attitudes, choices and beliefs. They do different things for different reasons.

If you are between the ages of 34 and 52, you are part of a generation called "Boomers." You've been labeled as such because you were born during the baby boom that occurred immediately after the last world war. You are considered a Boomer if you were born between the years 1946 and 1964.

By sheer numbers, Boomers have dominated, and they are central to other generations. So much so, that others are socially defined in terms of their relationship to Boomers.

If you were born before 1946 you are known as Parents-of- Boomers or Those-Born-Before-Boomers. If you were born after 1965 you have been given various names — Echo Generation, Boomer-Bust, Generation X, to name a few — but you are nonetheless commonly thought of as Children-of-Boomers or Those-Born-After-Boomers.

In the United States there are roughly 76 million so-called Boomers. In Canada the number has been estimated to be in the neighborhood of 9 million. This is significantly less than the United States, but if you factor in that this number represents 33 percent of the total population of Canada, you can begin to appreciate the impact Boomers have on the Canadian economy. The mass alone of Boomers has had an enormous impact on the national psyche, political arena and social fabric. Boomers have been the catalyst to many changes.

In the 1960s and 1970s Boomers created a youth culture never before experienced in society. Flower Power was everywhere. And so were anti-war demonstrations, shocking hemlines and loud rock and roll music. Love, Peace and Happiness was the collective youth mantra. This generation of youth, unlike any that preceded it, had a voice. Because of the sheer numbers (there had never been so many young people in society at the same time), it was a loud voice.

The Boomer generation continued using their voice and the power of their numbers. As they did in their youth, Boomers reinterpreted each successive stage of life as they went through it. They produced the dual-income households of the 1980s and 1990s, and it redefined the family unit.

Gone were the days of the previous generation's ideal of 'mom at home'. Replacing her were career-moms, super-moms, divorced moms and step-moms. Entwined with step-sisters, step-brothers and step-dads, the average family unit defies description. Boomers have reinvented the family unit and will be reinventing retirement in the 21st Century.

Boomers are big business.

For years, companies have focused on strategies to attract Boomer dollars. When Boomers hit a market, they hit *hard*. Because of this, they have been a favorite topic in boardrooms across North America. Many corporate strategies have begun with the question, "What are Boomers heading for next, and how can we get a piece of the action?"

Boomers gave birth to the concept of mass marketing. Industry has courted Boomers ever since their power in the marketplace was first noticed by a company called Gerber.

Gerber makes baby food, and as the boomers came into this world, demand for their product rose with each birth. Gerber immediately felt the impact on their bottom line. More babies meant more demand for their product. More demand meant more baby food could be sold. With a strategy of clever marketing, sales soared.

Consumerism is Born With Boomers

Boomers are a big and complex group. As a group, they are a generation that openly and vocally lauds individuality. Yet ironically, Boomers are a group that act like a collective. They all want the same things, which is whatever is hot and popular. Regardless of how or why, Boomers frequently cause the marketplace to shape itself to cater to their unique, yet generational priorities and wants.

We've seen it so many times over the years. During the 1970s, the music industry flourished. Who bought all the albums that fueled the music industry? Boomers. In the 1980s the real estate industry went through an unprecedented boon time. Who was buying all the houses? Boomers. Look at the recent decade of success within the automobile industry with mini vans and SUVs. Who bought them? Boomers.

This collective behavior of Boomers keeps industry licking its proverbial lips. And after all these years, marketers find few mysteries to reaching them. They know that appealing to Boomers' egos, for example, will usually result in a direct hit. Boomers find it hard to resist a marketing message that makes any of the following claims:

Three Things that Make a Boomer Want to Buy

1. The product will make them look younger.

2. A product will help them *appear* more attractive or more successful.

3. It offers "instant" gratification.

And if the product being marketed can claim to be "the most popular" or "best selling," you can usually gain a Boomer's trust and confidence. Boomers may claim individualism, but they usually want to buy what everyone else has bought. In my opinion, Boomers exhibit a herd mentality. They move with whatever is in the prevailing wind. Few Boomers will ever agree or admit to it, but that sure is what it looks like.

Different Generations make Different Choices

With the new century came a new reality. Beginning in the year 2000, there will be more teens and twenty-somethings than any other time in history. Even more than Boomers. The Echo Boom is poised to take over.

And what a difference a few years and a new generation can make. It is a very different playing field when marketing to the younger generations. The boomer-bust, Echo and Generation Xers are all notoriously jaded and cynical about advertising. They enjoy the artistry of ads but don't want to feel manipulated. At the first whiff of manipulation, they run away fast.

31

"People in this age group are very media savvy," coaches a prominent creative director in Toronto. "If you look like some big corporation selling them something, they will call bull. So you have to get under their radar."

A classic example of getting under their radar was recently engaged in the promotion of a new battery produced by Panasonic. The target market was Canadian youth, and research showed they buy the most batteries and are receptive to new brands. The creative team in charge of marketing knew that a full frontal assault-style media blitz was not the place to start. That often works for Boomers, but they have found it alienates younger generations.

Instead, they cleverly infiltrated the market and gained youth mindshare for months before the first television commercial aired. How? They selected DJs in five cities across Canada and offered them state-of-the-art Panasonic turntables — free. All the DJs had to do was distribute free hats, t-shirts and stickers with the PA logo on them during designated party nights. There was no mention of batteries, no mention of what PA meant or stood for, or who was promoting what. Even the DJs were not told. They just handed out the promotional material per their agreement. They were happy to oblige, as they were given the free equipment for their trouble.

At the same time as the DJ campaign, PA posters and stickers with images of speakers blown out began mysteriously showing up on construction site walls. Still no mention of any battery. But the logo had been carefully designed to be "cool" in the opinion of the young market that Panasonic was seeking. It worked. When the first television commercial aired months later, PA already had mindshare. It was already familiar to the intended market and had been accepted. It is no coincidence that market share follows mindshare. McDonald's knew this 99 billion burgers ago.

Boomers and Retirement

According to the US Census Bureau, the number of persons aged 65 years and over could more than double by the middle of this century. This will result in a huge demographic shift.

"The outlook is rosy" is the gleeful proclamation of pharmaceutical companies, private medical services, biotechnology, long-term care providers, internet pharmacies, couriers (from the burgeoning number of online purchases) and others poised take advantage of an aging population. And for good reason.

It is predicted that tomorrow's seniors will be among the healthiest and most active ever. Not only were Boomers the largest demographic group ever in North America, they will also be the first to reap the benefits of all the improvements in medicine and technology that took place at the end of the century. As a whole, this group will have a longer life span than any previous generation.

Boomers will continue to command the attention of demographers, politicians, marketers, social scientists and economists. They all are curious as to where the behemoth of Boomers is heading next, because wherever it is, money is to be made. And wherever there is money to be made, you will find a lot of focused energy. You'll also find a lot of marketing and advertising.

Predictions are Rampant

Pundits and gurus have never been busier as they try to figure out the next Boomer moves. Whatever happens, there is one fact we can all rely upon— Boomers are getting older. And as much as they would like to, this fact can not be denied. Sooner or later, they are all heading for retirement.

When asked, Boomers cite traveling as the activity most looked forward to in their retirement. If they are able to travel as much as they'd like to (note that it is an activity they most look forward to, not a confirmation of the existence of the ability to pay for it) then *maybe* there is just cause for hoteliers, airlines, tour companies and associated businesses to eagerly anticipate receiving many Boomer retirement dollars.

The financial services industry also expects their business to flourish. I agree there is a certain logic to the recent landslide of books from this sector predicting Boomers pouring unprecedented mountains of money into their investment portfolios. After all, as a group they are in the ages when serious saving typically occurs. It will be a good thing if Boomers do succeed in accumulating wealth. A very, very good thing. Because it will mean that they actually have the financial wherewithal to have an independent retirement.

But since Boomers have zero history of doing the typical, what reason on earth do we have to believe that this time will be different? Their generational trademark has been in redefining. If anything is predictable about Boomers, it is their tendency to redefine.

They are off to a pretty good start at redefining retirement. Most of them say they plan to work longer, because they know they are going to live longer. This will certainly redefine the workplace and the meaning of retirement years. But this may not be the biggest change they affect regarding retirement. *There is disturbing evidence that Boomers are woefully unprepared for their impending retirement.*

In the mid 1990s, when the initial buzz about retiring Boomers began, there were many upbeat reports. According to the Congressional Budget Office (CBO), Boomers were doing better than their parents were at the same age. Their household income was higher and they had a higher wealth to income ratio. Researchers at Cornell University estimated that Boomers would inherit $10.4 trillion over the next 50 years, or an average bequest of $90,200. And many of them had equity in their homes to add to optimism that "Boomers were in good shape."

But there were a few erroneous assumptions included in these initial assessments, as pointed out in a Retirement Planning Supplement produced toward the end of the decade. For the predictions to play out, real wages would have to grow faster than prices during the next 20 to 40 years, tax and benefit policies would have to remain unchanged, and parents would have to pass on substantial assets with no costs of death and no asset erosion for estate taxes. Basically, it meant that Boomers would be okay. . . in an ideal world.

Have you ever noticed how frequently there is a gap between the ideal world and the real world? Retirement predictions for Boomers may be no exception.

Few Boomers are Prepared, Many are Narcissistic

A Boomer turns 50 every 7.5 minutes in the United States. That's 11,000 a day. But few of them will retire soon, experts now say. They won't be able to afford it.

If they've been thinking about retirement at all, they certainly haven't been planning for it. According to the US Public Agenda, 38 percent of Boomers say they have less than $10,000 in any form of savings. Only 16 percent say they have $100,000 or more in savings for retirement. That means it is quite possible that almost half of Boomers in North America have absolutely no personal savings for retirement!

These are the years that many predicted the Boomers would be really socking money away. Trust Boomers to defy tradition! And trust them to do it as a group.

If life is about the choices we make, Boomers have been making some rather peculiar choices. They have *chosen* not to save for the future. Remember when I said that when we make one decision we actually make quite a few? (If we choose to go to Palm Desert, for example, we in effect chose not to go to Spain or Chicago, etc.) Well it is the same thing here. If we choose to spend it, we can not save it. If we don't save it we can't invest it.

As they choose where their dollars go each year, Boomers choose not to save many, if any, for the future. Hard-working, high-earning Americans are finding themselves living paycheck to paycheck in their hot pursuit of the middle-class dream.

So what happened to the old-fashioned notion of living within your means and buying only what you need? Many experts including family and marriage counselors believe a barrage of advertising targeted at the middle and upper middle classes, which tells us what we just can't do without, is largely responsible for the "because-I'm-worth-it" mentality.

And this 'I must have it all' attitude often leads to money troubles. Unrestrained consumerism has forced many people to seek help and frequently these are people making $150,000 plus per year.

Feeling overworked and burdened by debt, the pressure can be enormous. Advertising creates needs that people were not even aware they had. But if you succumb to it, you can easily feel entitled to redecorate your home every five years or that you are denying a basic human right if you don't have a new car every three years. The emphasis is on getting, buying and spending, rather than standing back and saying, "Is this a real need?" We're impulse driven, and increasingly narcissistic.

These attitudes cause well-educated and ambitious people to live beyond their means, and sociologists say they are treating more and more of the 'poor rich' for financial stress. Many therapists blame the cash-flow conundrum of their patients on a sense of entitlement, a feeling among even the moderately well-off that they ought to have it all.

If you look around objectively, you will see ample examples of people who seem to think they can go on spending and spending, on big cottages, gorgeous homes, or whatever they may or may not have the money to pay for.

Lack of money to pay for these items is no impediment to acquiring them. If we want it now, we can have it. Credit is easy to get. We've become an increasingly narcissistic society that feels not only entitled to everything we want, but that we deserve it.

Ouch. It is not flattering to say that as a society we are narcissistic. In my opinion, advertising has played a major role in creating this atmosphere. Regardless, the end result is a downwardly destined upwardly mobile middle-class who have little saved for retirement.

> *"When your outgo exceeds your income,*
> *your upkeep is your downfall."*
> —Anonymous

Youth are Making Different Choices

Interestingly, Boomer children are behaving quite differently from their parents. The "Baby-Bust" and "Echo" and Generation Xers that follow the Boomers are making different choices. They have different attitudes. They may pierce unmentionable body parts, and listen to weird (sound familiar?) music, but these young people are already socking money away!

Nearly 64 percent of Americans aged 18 to 34 are actually saving for retirement, according to recent surveys. And among those who are saving, the average age they began investing is 23. This is a full 13 years earlier than most current retirees 65 and older began saving. When surveyed, half of the Boomers' children are beginning to save for retirement before the age of 25. A remarkable 18 percent are doing so before they even hit 20, the report states.

RETIREMENT SAVINGS ACCORDING TO AGE

Retirement Savings	Overall	Young Adults Ages 22-32	Boomers Ages 33-50	Pre-Retirees Ages 51-61
$0	15%	22%	12%	13%
$1,000 - $9,999	31%	47%	26%	17%
$10,000 - $49,000	24%	18%	28%	20%
$50,000 - $99,999	13%	7%	16%	17%
$100,000 ⬩	15%	5%	16%	29%

Note: Figures do not add up to 100% because of rounding and answers of "Don't know" are not included. Source: Public Agenda

Their Boomer parents may prize instant gratification, but young generations are prepared to sacrifice to save money. A whopping 45 percent say they are willing to eat out less, 33 percent are willing to cut back on vacations and 25 percent would take a second job in order to adequately prepare for their retirement.

In sharp contrast, when Boomers earning more than $75,000 per year were asked if they are likely to cut back on vacation or travel expenses or do more careful grocery shopping to bolster their retirement savings, over 50 percent said "no." They seem to be firmly entrenched in their shop-til-you-drop and spend-til-you-bend tendencies. Unlike their children, Boomers prefer a more "live for today" lifestyle.

The younger generations are doing with their money what their Boomer parents couldn't or wouldn't or won't. Perhaps we shouldn't be surprised. Youth has always rebelled against their parents. That is, after all, what youth is all about — to challenge the "old" and find "new" ways. Boomers were no exception, and apparently neither are their kids. While Boomers may not want to be like their parents, maybe it might be a good idea for them to try acting like their children when it comes to saving money. The younger generation are the ones who seem to already know that tomorrow never lies.

"Grandchildren are God's way of compensating us for growing old."

— Mary H. Waldrop

Chapter 2 Review

- Our choices are inextricably linked with our attitudes.

- Each generation makes different choices and holds different attitudes.

- If you want to sell something to Boomers, tell them it will make them look younger, appear more attractive and successful or offer instant gratification.

- The marketing tactics that work so well on Boomers fail miserably with younger generations.

- Boomers' choices and attitudes have made them woefully unprepared for their impending retirement.

- Younger generations are way ahead of Boomers when it comes to savings. They have different attitudes and make different choices.

Chapter Three

The 7 Dangerous Money Myths

Chapter Three

❧

The 7 Dangerous Money Myths

*"You pity a man who is lame or blind,
but you never pity him for being a fool,
which is often a much greater misfortune."*
— Sidney Smith

Whatever the Life Plan you end up creating for yourself in later chapters, I know one thing for sure. It is going to take money. It is an undeniable fact that we need money to sustain ourselves on this planet, regardless of how simply we like to live. And if we prefer a lifestyle with a few more frills and perks, well, that just means more money. It's not that complicated.

Neither is getting it. Employment statistics confirm that most of us are indeed, gainfully employed. Sure, there is always a certain percentage of unemployed persons, but you must admit it is small compared to the numbers in the work force. If you want to earn money, you can find work.

Getting money is relatively easy. Keeping it is another matter. Anyone raising a family these days is acutely aware that money can seemingly vanish between deposits in the bank account. Hanging on to money can be hard.

And growing it so that we have an abundant (even sufficient) harvest at the end of the rainbow when we retire is quite another matter. That's where it gets complicated. I know, because that's the business I'm in — helping people like you grow investment portfolios designed to achieve personal retirement goals. The objective is to grow a 'nest egg' sufficient for the retirement lifestyle desired.

For nearly two decades now I've been doing this, and I've learned that there are many things that can get in the way of achieving the desired end result. Some are unavoidable. Some things happen that we can do nothing about; they are outside our control. But not all of them fall into this category. In fact most of them are something else. Literally.

In my work I have encountered seven common fallacies that prevent many good folks from achieving their retirement objectives. These fallacies are dangerous and entirely preventable.

I thought it might be effective to deal with some of these up front with you before we go on. In future chapters we will be delving into the concept of creating your own personal Life Plan. A good Life Plan, as you will see, takes unwavering commitment. That won't be forthcoming if you are hanging on to some dangerous beliefs, such as those that follow. Any of them will surely get in your way.

Dangerous Myth #1:

"The equity in my home will be my retirement."

"I will be fine in retirement because of my home equity," is a good example of the kind of thinking that will get you in trouble. Because it is simply not true. Equity on your primary residence is not a retirement nest egg. It is your home. It is where you live. Since you have to live somewhere, positioning your primary residence as a retirement fund puts you in a precarious position, to say the least.

Who says you will want to sell your home for living expenses when you are older? (Other than the advertisements of senior-style condominium developments.) More importantly, do you want to be *forced* to sell your home for living expenses? Or be driven to take out a Reverse Mortgage? For all intents and purposes, reverse mortgaging means tendering your home back to the bank. I consider it is a shame that the bank makes money on your way in, and then makes it again on the way out through reverse mortgages.

I think it is wise to arrange your affairs so that at least you have the choice. You can sell your house and move to wherever, or stay where you are, because you have the choice. When the time comes to retire, you may very well decide you like living in the family home and want to stay. Many new retirees today wouldn't think of selling their family home immediately upon retirement. Why would you assume you will? Just because the ads say so? Not a very good reason, if you ask me.

The myth that home equity was enough for retirement is not as common as it used to be. Most people now realize that it takes more than the equity on one single house to establish financial security. The myth grew out of a time when inflation was a homeowner's life long friend.

A good example is Grandpa and Grandma who bought the ranch for $10,000 in the 1930s. At that time, it was considered a hefty sum of money. But forty years and a couple of subdivisions later, and voila! One very comfortable retirement nest egg could be realized. Years of high inflation had an influence — what you could buy for a dollar had changed.

It is not just the value of a dollar that has changed. The world has changed. What it will be like when you retire is anybody's guess. Market values may hold, they may not. Your home may be worth more than it is today, and it is even possible that it will be worth less. Some futurists have suggested there may be no demand for the kind of home you have, in which case it could be unsaleable. Hard to imagine, isn't it? But then, in 1979 it was hard to imagine the wired world we would have to come to grips with only a short decade later.

Unless you are talking about a real estate portfolio with an inventory of revenue properties, you are kidding yourself thinking that your real estate ownership will be a suitable retirement nest egg. Unless you plan to live on the substance of a hummingbird's egg.

As I said, I think the majority of people realize that they will need to do more than buy a house to be prepared for retirement. Most people understand this. But it doesn't help when those who don't, read published articles that say if Boomers include home equity in their personal wealth, they have almost 85 percent of the amount needed to maintain their lifestyle in retirement. Figures like that may have misled some Boomers into thinking they didn't need to build savings and investment accounts, as statistics show that few have done so.

There is a big problem with that 85 percent figure mentioned above. It is only that high IF home equity is included in the Boomers' financial picture. If it is not included, Boomers probably have only 33 percent of the amount needed to maintain their current lifestyle in retirement.

Including home equity in personal wealth produces a misleading picture. It is more realistic NOT to include the home equity, especially if you want to be able to stay in your home and not convert it into cash immediately upon retirement.

If you are a Boomer who is naively thinking that a bountiful retirement awaits out of your home equity, know this: It is unlikely to happen that way.

Dangerous Myth #2:

"I will inherit my parents' money, so I don't have to worry."

Are you sure? If inheriting your parent's money is your whole retirement strategy, you may have a great deal to worry about. Many Boomers are counting heavily on receiving an inheritance. If this includes you, brace yourself for a news flash: It might not be there. Or it might not be quite the bundle you think it is. It might not even be close.

There are several reasons why. . .

First of all, people are living longer. Even longer than expected. Life expectancy increases three months every year. The latest actuarial figures now show that if a couple lives to 65 years of age, it is highly likely that one of them will make it to at least age 93. So, bluntly put, they'll be spending the money on life. You know — food, shelter, clothing and taxes. Plus whatever else comprises their lifestyle.

You've all seen the bumper stickers on RVs that say "I'm spending my kids' inheritance!" Some of them aren't joking! And, bless their hearts, Grandma and Grandpa are discovering many other, enjoyable ways to spend their money. Vacations in warmer climates. Golf junkets. Grandchildren. Visits to casinos. You know the stuff. And you also know how quickly living expenses such as those mentioned can add up over the years. And did I mention taxes?

And then there are the medical expenses. It is well known that as we age our medical needs and costs increase. As a rule, the longer we live, the larger the costs become. And as medical costs escalate, the 'inheritance' is directly effected.

Take Mr. & Mrs. B for example. I've known them for 14 years. The last time I met with Mr. B it wasn't a joyous meeting. Mr. B was feeling quite low. First of all, he missed his wife. At 92 and 88 years of age, their health had declined. Mr. B lived in a different care home than his wife, and according to him the food was gawd-awful in either place.

Mrs. B's condition required that she have more medical attention, which is why she lives in a different care home. They have $900,000 invested, but they want it as secure as possible, which at today's rates means 6 percent. That's $54,000 per year (he still has to pay taxes) and it's not really enough to cover expenses for both of them in two separate facilities, even before considering inflation.

Shortly before our last meeting he had come to the realization that for the first time in his life, he would have to spend some of his principal. He was really, really unhappy about it.

"It was truly viewed as a sin all those years. But now it's become a necessity," he said, referring to his need to dip into their principal. He hated doing that. He had intended to leave it to his two daughters and five grandchildren. But interest alone no longer provided sufficient funds for Mr. B. to take care of himself, and his beloved Mrs. B.

Another element that is taking chunks out of seniors' life savings is unsavory. There are, and have always been, plenty of con artists and their smooth talking swindler cousins. A number of them target seniors, and prey on their vulnerability. And take their money — lots of it. These are heinous crimes that often go undetected. We have no real way of calculating the amounts scooped by fraudulent means because many seniors are too embarrassed to tell anyone. But it is a fact, folks, across this country many, many overly trusting seniors have had their life savings, or a substantial part of them, duped away by fraud artists.

There are more reasons why Boomers who are counting on receiving an inheritance from their parents may be setting themselves up for some serious disappointment. They are called girlfriends, men friends, new husbands and new wives. And maybe even whole new families. If you think it won't happen in your family, maybe you should think again. It has happened to many that never, ever thought it would.

For example, I have a 48 year old client who didn't think it would ever happen to her family. But life played out differently than she expected. She had to watch her father spend her inheritance on a girlfriend after her mother died. I remember the day she came into my office in tears because her father had just confessed that he'd spent himself into debt and she would get no money. Barbara was a very unhappy lady with a lot of catching up to do for her retirement savings. As might anyone who is counting on retiring with their parent's money.

Dangerous Myth #3:

"There will be safety in numbers."

Just because there are plenty of other people with insufficient money for retirement, it doesn't mean there will be safety in numbers. If you are thinking "Well, all of us will be in the same boat, so somebody will have to do something," I advise you to think of the Titanic. The Titanic was a pretty big boat, and we all know the end to that story.

Perhaps there is safety in numbers when walking home at night. But there is little safety in numbers when you are on a sinking ship. In fact, the more people on the sinking ship, the harder it is to have a seat in a lifeboat for everyone. I assume we all have seen the movie or at least know the Titanic story. There were not enough lifeboats for all the passengers in a needful predicament. As the ship went down, there was nothing that any one could do. There was no safety in numbers.

Counting on things being okay, simply because there are many others like you, is a dangerous myth. The tragic consequences of dogmatism throughout history was summed up quite well by the noteworthy Bertrand Russell when he said, "Most of the greatest evils that man has inflicted upon man have come through people feeling quite certain about something which, in fact, was false."

"There are more horses asses than there are horses."
—Anonymous

Dangerous Myth #4:

"I am so far behind in my investment plans that I must take excessive risks in order to catch up."

This kind of dangerous thinking is prevalent among many Boomers who haven't sufficiently prepared for retirement. In an effort to counteract what they haven't accomplished, they swarm to the highest risk investments and hope for the highest returns. (Which, by the way, repeatedly produces the exact opposite of the desired result.) There is a lot of money being lost because of this hazardous thinking, but it's not just the Boomers trying to catch up who are losing.

Take, for example, Alan G. He's 58 years of age and in his own words "tired as hell of being a realtor." Two years ago Alan and his wife split. She got the house and the cottage, and Alan's portion was roughly $750,000.

Fuming over the fact that his wife "got half his money," Alan adopted the dangerous thinking stated above. Alan felt that he had to make up for it, and he caught a dose of high tech mania. He promptly put half of his savings into one such stock (quite possibly recommended to him at a cocktail party). Alan had obviously not learned that an overly emotional state is a poor one in which to make major decisions. Within a short period of time the stock plummeted in value, and Alan abruptly lost half his money. That wiped out the first $300,000.

Now even more anxious to make up for what he perceived as lost ground, Alan felt desperate. He put what he had left into another highly speculative tech stock. (Another thing Alan obviously didn't know was that by the time you spot a bandwagon, the window of opportunity is usually closed.) A close friend of his had made a significant amount of money on this stock and Alan naively (or stupidly) crossed his fingers and hoped the same would happen to him. It did not. Two years after his divorce, Alan was in my office and talking suicide.

"I've lost it all," he informed me mournfully. "I don't know what I'm going to do now . . ."

Alan had rolled the dice twice and in doing so, had lost $700,000. Understandably, he was having a hard time living with the consequences of his actions. It is not easy to forgive oneself for blowing nearly three quarters of a million dollars. It is not easy with *any* amount of money, if that amount is all you have.

54

Use the Choke 'n Poke Strategy

What Alan should have done two years ago is adopt what I call a Choke and Poke strategy. Instead of trying to hit a home run, he should have been more concerned about getting on base. Hitting singles may not be sexy, but it gets you around the bases and you stay in the game. It may take a little longer to reach home plate, but the likelihood of success with this strategy is so much higher. For reasons why, we can look to Babe Ruth — the beloved champion of home runs.

Babe Ruth's Stats

Year	Home Runs	Strike Outs
1918	*11	58
1923	41	93
1924	46	81
1927	60	89
1928	54	87

This number is correct! In 1918, Babe Ruth led the league with only 11 home runs.

There is no question Babe Ruth had a stellar record. In five regular seasons, he led the league in home runs. But if you study all his stats, you'll see a pattern emerge. *He also led the league in strike outs.*

Hockey-gifted Pavel Bure frequently leads his team (if not the entire league) in goals. He also registers the most shots taken. Which means, *he also leads in shots missed!* Michael Jordan led the NBA in buzzer beaters. *He also led the league in missed buzzer beaters.*

I could go on and on with examples. The point is, we think only about the triumphs of others. The other side of that very real coin are the missed attempts. Please note that they *always* exceed the wins. More shots are missed than made. This is fine and dandy for professional athletes. They are paid to do this. The Babe Ruth analogy does not work for investing. No one can stay in the investment game if they consistently miss more shots than they make.

The secret to investing is to get on base every time rather than going for the home run. Don N. and his wife Luanne made the same mistake as our friend Alan, the divorced realtor. In an attempt to hit a home run, they invested a whopping 64 percent of their assets in a high flying precious metal fund. So far on their $131,837 investment, they have lost $62,464. They have lost half their money. It only took them four years to lose it.

But that's only half the pain.

The other half of the pain is the opportunity cost of such treacherous decisions gone awry. What else could they have done with this money?

Had they tried to get on base rather than going for the home run stock or mutual fund, they could have used compounding to their advantage. At a 10 percent rate of return, that money would have grown to $191,797. Instead, it is now worth $69,373. If you look at it this way, they have lost a total of $122,424. That is the amount that they have lost if you include the opportunity cost.

That is often the price paid when you risk too much going for the home run stock. I think it is wiser to shorten up your swing and hit singles. Hence, the name Choke 'n Poke.

Dangerous Myth #5:

"I'm looking forward to early retirement. I have nothing to worry about."

I wish everyone who felt this way had good reasons to be so sure. The reality, in my experience, is that many of you don't.

My staff and I have often been in the position of breaking the news to people who hadn't seriously planned for it, but were approaching the time they thought they might like to retire. They assumed they could. But once we crunch the numbers, there is often a huge gap between what they will have and what they will need in order to retire with their anticipated lifestyle. Retirement must be delayed. This is not easy news to deliver.

But there may be even more unhappy news on the horizon for some people who have already retired. I immediately think of an stubborn 65-year-old by the name of Tommy W. He has already retired, sold his house and downsized. Today his portfolio is worth about $575,000 and none of it is in fixed income. He doesn't think he needs asset allocation. He thinks there is no potential whatsoever for a market meltdown of even 20 percent. Tommy thinks he has nothing to worry about.

If Tommy is wrong, he has plenty to worry about. A market downturn would have a severe impact on his monthly income. But Tommy is stubborn, and refuses to make any changes to his portfolio to insulate himself. Does he consider himself invincible?

Many Boomers will run out of money by age 85, according to some experts. Many who will run out of money are people who dreamed of retiring at age 55, never having to think about it again.

It is not easy to break the news of this reality to people in their late forties and early fifties. Many are finding out they must work until at least their sixties (or beyond), and they aren't too happy about it. And for many, the news gets worse. If they maintain their current spending habits, they won't have a chance of having enough money at 85. Not unless the market returns reach unachievable fantasy targets.

So, if you are coasting along on a comfort zone that tells you there is nothing to worry about, make sure you get it validated by a professional Financial Advisor. He or she may not have news you want to hear, but the sooner you hear it the better. The day you wish to retire is not the day to visit a financial professional. I have noticed that many people spend more time planning their annual vacation than they do their financial affairs. Make an appointment with a competent professional sooner rather than later.

Dangerous Myth #6:

"I've got plenty of time. I'm in no hurry to retire. I'll start my investment plan later."

Have you not heard of the c-o-m-p-o-u-n-d-i-n-g effect? It is never, ever too soon to start.

Having said that, it is highly probable that many Boomers will be working longer into their lives than their parents did. According to research, many Boomers say they plan to work past the official retirement age. A recent study by the American Association of Retired Persons indicated that 90 percent of Boomers plan to work past 65, either to reduce boredom or because of financial necessity.

This is all fine and dandy providing two things also occur.

First of all, the jobs must be there. This may well be the case, there might be an abundance of jobs available for you, but I question the wisdom of counting on it as a sure thing. How can you be so sure?

We have all seen companies pare themselves down to minimal staff, either because of economic necessity or the introduction of new technology. It doesn't seem likely that the trend is going to reverse itself anytime soon. As technology keeps speeding ahead, each year fewer and fewer workers are required to get the job done. So where will all the jobs be? Doing what? And remember that whatever jobs there are, millions of young people will also be competing for them.

Secondly, you must remain perfectly healthy in order to be able to keep working. If any medical problems arise, then what? It is no secret that health often declines with age. The older we get, the higher the likelihood of medical conditions popping up.

And let's face it, as a society we do not have a reputation for doing the things we know would help keep us healthy. Despite a burgeoning weight loss industry, fitness clubs, and all the information readily available, as a society we aren't in very good shape. An estimated 55 percent of U.S. adults are now overweight and a whopping 23 percent are considered obese. One in five American children are now classified as overweight.

Canadians are not far behind. An estimated 48 percent of adult Canadians are overweight, and about 14 percent of adults and a growing number of children are obese. It makes me wonder if we will be healthy enough to keep working into our retirement years, as we plan.

I certainly understand wanting to work, even if financial conditions don't require it, and health permits it. It's great to feel productive and that you are contributing in some way, at any age. This was evidenced recently when I walked into The Gap and discovered a fellow I knew from my tennis club happily employed there. He is nearly 70 years old! Why was he working?

"Something to do!" was the immediate reply when I asked.

Like I said, I understand wanting to work. But no one can count on being able to do so with any certainty. Once again, it is better to cover your bases and make sure that you have the choice. And it is never too soon to start.

"A man's treatment of money is the most decisive test of his character — how he makes it and how he spends it."
—James Moffatt

Dangerous Myth #7:

"There is nothing I can do. I've left it too long and now there is not enough time and/or there is not enough money left over at the end of the month to save."

First of all, it is never too late to start. And secondly, there is always something you can do — if you choose. It is your decision to make. It is *always* your decision to make.

It reminds me of the story of the 45 year old, recently unemployed but given a fairly decent severance package (corporate downsizing after a takeover). The man was pondering his future and mentioned that he'd always wanted to be a lawyer. After investigating the educational program at his local university, the man discovered that it would take him seven years to earn his law degree. Discussing it the next day with his wife, he lamented that he didn't think it was feasible.

"It's too late," he said. "I'll be 52 years old in seven years when I finally graduate."

"And how old will you be in seven years if you don't go?" his astute wife asked pointedly.

She makes a good point.

In seven years, he will be 52 years old, no matter what he does. So his choice is simple. Either he is 52 years old with the law degree he always wanted. Or he can be 52 years old without it — and wishing he had gone for it.

It is never too late to do what you need or want to do.

If you haven't yet started your financial plan, no matter what your age, start now. You will be 85 or 95 (or older) some day, whether or not you plan for it. Just like the fellow who would be 52 years old in seven years whether or not he studied for his law degree. In the meantime, use each year wisely.

Tomorrow never lies.

There is always something you can do.

Now, about that business of not having any money left over at the end of the month to save. Nonsense! I can almost guarantee you that, starting this month, you can be putting away money you never thought you had. If you want to find it, you can.

A typical household today has two incomes, is saving for their children's college expenses, caring for their aging parents and find saving for the future an ideology. Families are burdened with taxes (especially in Canada), enduring incessant stress from all directions and feeling like there aren't enough hours in the day to even think about twenty years from now, let alone be putting money away for it. The household lives under heavy debt and from payday to payday. Sound familiar? If it does, you know you are not alone. It is familiar to the majority of households today. It is easy to find it difficult to save money.

Almost 70 percent of workers of all ages say they could save more for retirement if they cut back on expenses. Yet they are reluctant to do so, preferring more of a "live for today" lifestyle.

For a word from one of the most competent women I know on the subject of managing household money, let me introduce you to a lady by the name of Margaret. She and her husband are in their early to mid-forties with two children. She is a school teacher, he is an engineer. Both make average salaries.

They manage their money well. Extremely well. They own a nice house in a good area of Vancouver, travel, and their investment portfolio of over $200,000 is well invested. I asked her directly one day, how she does it. Margaret's answer was quick and just as direct: "It's simple — we don't live beyond our means."

Chapter 3 Review

The Dangerous Money Myths are:

1. The equity in my home will be my retirement.

2. I will inherit my parents' money, so I don't have to worry.

3. There will be safety in numbers.

4. I am so far behind in my investment plans that I must take excessive risks in order to catch up.

5. I'm looking forward to early retirement. I have nothing to worry about.

6. I've got plenty of time. I'm in no hurry to retire. I'll start my investment plan later.

7. There is nothing I can do. I've left it too long and now there is not enough time and/or there is not enough money left over at the end of the month to save.

Chapter Four

~

Our Secret Weapons

Chapter Four

❧

Our Secret Weapons:

Attitudes & Words

"Attitude is a little thing that makes a big difference."
—Anonymous

*"Words are the dress of our thoughts which should
no more be presented in rags, tatters and dirt than
your person should."*
—Lord Chesterfield

In life, think of attitude as a wild card, an ace up your sleeve. Because in the game of life, attitude is what levels the playing field. It is like the legend of Samson's hair; it gives a winning advantage in an otherwise hopeless situation.

For anyone and everyone who wants to really get in the game of life, and come out victorious, attitude is your most useful and powerful tool. It doesn't matter which generation you are part of, or how old you are, or what your particular situation is right now, your attitude is your silent partner and your silent power. Attitude is what separates winners from losers and wanna-be's.

It's free, it's yours and you can make it anything you want it to be. You can change it whenever you want, or not at all. It is all up to you. How important is attitude? Well, let me ask you this — how important is something that effects how you think, feel and act? It is my experience that our attitude affects, if not outright determines, our thoughts, feelings and actions (and/or reactions).

Take the war on stress, for example.

Stress seems to be everyone's conversation. Stress is a popular subject of chat shows, both radio and television. Headlines on magazine and newspaper covers frequently make reference to it. I hear stress being talked about everywhere, by all ages. Business associates look at each other knowingly when the topic is brought up. Busy parents exchange "I-know-what-you-mean" glances outside their SUVs while waiting for, or dropping off children at school and other activities. Co-workers commiserate in lunchrooms, internet chat rooms and compare stress loads. Everyone is stressed! Even 10-year-olds speak of stress from personal experience.

Crimes of Haste

We are stressed because we think we don't have enough time. It seems that there are not enough hours in the day. We live in a hurry all the time, rushing here and there and cramming as many activities together as we can, in hopes of gaining some time. Time for our kids. Time to catch up on our reading, or sleep. Time for a golf game. Time to exercise. Time for each other. Time for ourselves. Oh, what we would do, if only we had more time!

Our quest to "save time" is relentless, and has produced some pretty razoo technology. Where it's going, we don't know because it seems that we already have it all wrapped up in one time or labor saving device after the other. How did we ever live without Palm Pilots that enable us to summon the internet as we walk down the street? Really.

But I'll bet we haven't seen anything yet, because enough is rarely enough for us humans.

Ever notice how impatient you can get waiting that 70 seconds to zap your oatmeal or instant coffee? Does anyone *not* pump the close button on the elevator if the door doesn't immediately do so? And crosswalk buttons! For years my office gave me a great view of an intersection that was a perpetual example of human impatience.

If the crosswalk button didn't produce the desired result immediately, it got tapped again. And again. And again. It got tapped, slapped, smacked and whacked until the light finally changed. Which, it always did, but only after the preprogrammed amount of time passed. It really didn't matter how many times the button was pressed, it still took the same amount of time to change from 'don't walk' to "walk.' I think we all know this, but it doesn't deter us from fruitlessly trying to speed things along. We like speed.

If our computer hesitates for a nanosecond before delivering our latest search request, we start drumming our fingers. Things are only fast enough for us if they are instant.

Not all of us feel that way, thank goodness. There is at least one elderly gentleman in Vancouver, Canada who feels differently. He was waiting for an elevator the other day in a lovely old, historical building, as was a friend of mine. Finally a car arrived and they both got in and pushed the buttons for the floors to which they wished to be taken.

After a lengthy hesitation, the old elevator rumbled and fumbled into action. It was a slow elevator, as could be expected for its vintage. My friend was in a big hurry that day (as usual!) and muttered something under his breath about how slow the elevator was, to which the gentle gray haired man smiled and said —

"Oh, I think the elevator is moving at the perfect speed. It's *us* that are trying to move at the wrong one."

The old gentleman makes a point. But it isn't shared by many.

Another friend of mine who had laser eye surgery shared with me just what lengths we will go to speed up a process at any cost. Here's the scenario:

The reception area was the "holding tank" for patients about to undergo the laser eye operation to improve their vision. The clinic offered a choice of procedures: tried, tested and proven PRK (photorefractive keratectomy) or the new lasik procedure referred to in medical circles as "flap 'n zap." The full sight recovery time for PRK was about a week, but the risk was minimal. The newer lasik procedure carried a much higher risk of complications, in that if they occurred, they were very serious. But the sight recovery time was faster. The cost to the patient was higher.

An amazing thing started happening as the patients were chatting in the waiting room comparing their procedure choices. When they discovered the other procedure's recovery time was faster, some PRK-destined patients abruptly wanted to change their choice. When the receptionist informed them that they could, if they were willing to pay the additional cost, they reacted as if they'd really scored big time. They asked no other questions, only if they could switch. Risk and cost instantly took a backseat to speed, in a two seater sports car. Isn't that interesting?

Now, I've been blessed with incredible vision all my life, so maybe I can't appreciate what's going on here. But I find it curious that anybody could be so nonchalant while rolling the dice with their ability to see. Just for the difference of a couple of days out of their entire life. Does speed always win just because it's faster?

And here's the real kicker of this story. Turns out the only reason lasik was more expensive was because it was more popular! More people wanted it, so they felt they could charge more. They were right. The faster recovery time was perceived as such a high value to potential patients, that the clinic could levy a higher price. This is interesting, because a high price is often attached to high risk when speed is also part of the equation.

This is not an isolated incident of a marketplace being exploited using speed as the "prize." I have long suspected that the computer industry routinely does this. With some well placed advertising and marketing, they are able to sell the latest and greatest (meaning faster) new models by convincing people that the computer they bought yesterday (or last year) is pathetically slow. It may only be slower by a fraction of a second, but when speed is king, that fraction of a second is all it takes to create a whole new market of eager purchasers.

Just because we all believe it, doesn't mean it's true.

Faster has become synonymous with better. It probably isn't true, but it is a commonly held belief. This wouldn't be the first time we've been wrong, collectively speaking. Throughout history, many commonly held beliefs ended up being untrue.

My staff and I were discussing this concept over lunch one day and everyone had input. We could all think of an example. My long time assistant, and much valued Michelle Jones shared a personal story of a false, but common misconception.

For about 20 years her husband, Ed thought he suffered from ulcers. Then one evening Ed watched *The Nature of Things,* a television show hosted by David Suzuki and learned that it was quite possible his 'ulcers' were caused by a bacteria.

Ed went back to his doctor. A specialist did the necessary tests, and Ed was treated for the bacteria that was, in fact, causing his "ulcers." When he went back a few weeks later for a follow up check up, Ed already knew what the doctors were going to say — "They (the ulcers) are gone!"

Hey, we used to believe the earth was flat! We also once believed that wearing fur was okay, that landfill sites were all we needed to manage our waste, pesticides and PCBs were welcome miracles, and that Dr. Spock knew everything about child-rearing. At one time we commonly believed that red wine was bad for you and that high impact aerobics were good. Well, now we've changed our collective minds and believe the reverse — that red wine is good and high impact exercise is bad.

Someday, we might change our minds about this business of faster being synonymous with better. For now, that attitude is a commonly held belief. And it is, I contend, at the root of much of the stress we feel. When speed is king, stress is his seductive queen. This royal couple will wreak royal havoc in our lives, if we choose to become their loyal subjects.

If we *choose* to believe the advertising pitches we are bombarded with daily, we can be made to feel inferior if we don't have whatever is proclaimed as the latest and greatest. Many Boomer parents seem to feel that if their kids don't have the latest and greatest, they are somehow being poor parents. Talk about stress! And all because of something that isn't true. But as a result of our choice to believe it to be true, we heap a whole pile of needless stress on ourselves. How much sense does this make? Not much!

Our obsession with speed must be driving manufacturers nuts as they scramble to accommodate us. Microwave bacon hit the grocery stores proclaiming to be ready in five seconds. That's fast, but not fast enough for one shopper at the sample kiosk.

"Mmmm. That's good," he said as he munched a piece. "But do you have anything faster?"

Multi-Tasking

Not only is haste our priority, we hate doing only one thing at a time. One of today's challenges seems to be finding how much we can do at the same time.

We chat on the phone while we read our e-mail. We watch television with a remote control in our hands while we sit with our laptops and surf the internet. The television industry is aware of these relatively new habits, and it makes them nervous. They remember what happened to radio.

When radio first came along the family was content to gather around and listen to whatever program was broadcasting. When the television came along with its visual candy, the radio was upstaged and relegated to the background. It became something that was on while we attended to other chores. By itself, the radio was no longer enough. The television was bells and whistles. Radio only whistled.

Well, now there's the internet and television is no longer enough to hold our attention on its own. As a result, those with a vested interest in the television industry are rapidly developing interactive technologies and other gadgets, hoping to recapture your attention. One thing at a time is no longer enough. As a society, we act as if we have collectively come down with a serious case of Attention Deficit Disorder. Time is our friend, and at the same time, is our enemy.

There is no question that time is valuable, but for some it has become a status symbol. If you can take off whenever you want to engage in some form of recreation, it means you have power. An abundance of it is considered to be bragging rights.

Sadly, in some circles time has become a negative status symbol. The less time we have available, the more status is perceived. Is this ever true for the average worker in Corporate America! Listen while middle managers negotiate a lunch appointment. Tell me there isn't a reluctance for either party to concede a more open, or available calendar. We seem to think the busier we are, the more important we are. Or more accurately, we hope we will be *perceived* as more important.

I realized that our obsession with time and speed had reached ridiculous levels when I heard about the One-Minute Bedtime Stories. The timing of this tidbit of news came shortly after I'd read a report that concluded reading to our children is perhaps one of the most important things we can do as a parent. The lifetime benefits are numerous, and include a comfortableness with intimacy, bonding, and a higher likelihood of the child doing better all through school, both socially and academically. Ergo: bedtime story reading is incredibly important. Yet, an entire series of One-Minute Bedtime Story books have been developed. And they sell!

Am I the only one that thinks we have really lost perspective? I can hardly believe that parents forego the simple (and so important) joy of reading a bedtime story to our child by convincing themselves that the one minute abbreviation is a par experience. I can't imagine what monumentally important activity that extra ten minutes allows us to do.

Attitude is Power

While some of us may long for society's return to a much simpler way, life seems to have its own ideas. Life seems to be moving at a pace that can leave even the most stalwart of us breathless at times, with no signs of it slowing down. That's reality.

So we need to learn to live with it. Manage it. Engage strategies so that stress has the least possible effect on us, our families and our lives. Govern our time. Regain some balance and perspective. Forget about commonly held false beliefs. Get our Plan for Life together. Not just talk about it, but actually do it.

It sounds like a tall order, but the good news is: It can be done! The power to do so exists at our fingertips with our attitudes. Attitudes have that kind of power.

If you ask people what things cause them stress, the list will include an impressive variety of villains ranging from the economy to their bosses, and just about everything else in between. But you know what? It isn't the event, activity, or person that causes our stress. Stress is determined by our *reaction* to the event, person or activity. And our reaction to it is determined by our *attitude*.

Our attitude determines how we *choose* to react. That's a mouthful, so let me explain using an extreme example — road rage.

Let's say you are cruising down the freeway and someone cuts you off, is going too slowly or whatever offense qualifies to get your attention. At the moment the 'inconsiderate' driver's action affects you, you make a choice. You can take a deep breath and remind yourself that this is no big deal, and that there is no need to allow yourself to be upset by this. You can forget about the other driver and carry on with your day. If you choose to do this, no stress occurs.

On the other hand, you can choose to become annoyed with the other driver. There are various levels of annoyance available, ranging from mild ("What a jerk!) to extreme ("Where-did-I-put-my-gun!). Regardless of the level, any choice of annoyance results in stress. The amount of stress is parallel in intensity to the level of annoyance. The more annoyed we feel, the higher the stress level we experience as a result.

Tipping the Dominoes

Once you make the choice to become annoyed (and therefore stressed) the dominoes of life begin to tip. One knocks the next one over. And that one knocks the next one, and so on. Beware the tipping domino effect! It can become quite lengthy. And as the dominoes tip, stress levels go higher and higher. Your blood pressure and your heart rate increase. Adrenalin rushes create an insulin imbalance, and on and on. There are many chemical reactions in the body that are triggered by stress. None of them are helpful to your overall health.

Until you make a new choice to drop the experience (mentally and emotionally), it will continue to tip your dominoes and induce more stress. If you don't let go, when you get home you might snap at your spouse, for example, and that can start a whole new row of dominoes falling. And then there's more stress. And more and more.

By maintaining control of our attitude, the stressful effect of a situation can be minimized, and maybe even eliminated altogether. It is all up to us. It is our choice to make. If, at any point, we recognize that we have lost control of our attitude, we can always choose to take it back. (And save ourselves from a potentially huge embarrassment of going off like a loose cannon.) We always have the choice.

> *" ANGER is one letter away from DANGER."*
> —Anonymous

I learned a good rule of thumb a few years ago regarding how to decide if something qualifies as a Big Deal. Before I take on the stress, I ask myself, "In five years will this matter?" Almost always, the answer is no. In fact, most situations can be dismissed by asking myself if it will matter *tomorrow*, never mind five years from now.

What Price for this Decision?

Every decision, every choice has a price or a consequence. It seems to be part of the rules. For every action there is an equal and opposite reaction, say the physicists. In life this translates into a consequence for an action. There is a price we pay for each choice we make. Sometimes the price we pay is immediate, but not always.

If we don't take control of our attitude in a road rage situation, and instead *decide* to allow ourselves to spin out of control, we could face serious future consequences. Flared tempers, hurled insults and a bit of property bashing are serious enough. In the most extreme, the price we pay could be manslaughter, and living with the horrible guilt.

This happens. One particularly awful case of road rage happened in Alabama in the fall of 1999. Two women, both around the age of 40 and both on their way home to their families after work, allowed themselves to get out of control to the point where one woman took a gun out of her glove box and shot and fatally injured (killed) the other. In a blink both their lives changed forever.

Perhaps even more tragic is the effect their decisions ultimately had on the loved ones and families of these women. One family's mother would never come home. She was dead. The other woman's family faced life without her too, and she herself faced a jail term. Everyone paid an extremely high price for the rest of their lives. All because of two split-second decisions, or choices made by two otherwise average working mothers.

The price paid for choices made was swift and immediate in this case of road rage. There was no doubt in

81

anyone's mind about the consequence of a foolish choice. I don't have to ask either of these ladies to know what they would do differently, if they had it all to do over again. I know their attitudes about the situation, had they known the price that was about to be paid, would have been different. They would have made different choices. Hindsight, it is said, is 20/20 vision.

Weeks later, callers discussing the incident on a radio talk show expressed sorrow at the tragedy, but many of them said it was "understandable." Yikes!

Sometimes the price we pay for a choice doesn't come for years and isn't so obvious. If our attitude is purely "Live for Today and Only Today" we will likely choose not to save and invest. We feel no immediate consequence for this attitude and choice. In fact, it can actually feel good — we have more money to spend today. But it's a foolish choice we'll pay a price for in the future. A high price. Tomorrow never lies.

Five Minutes that Make a Difference

I know what kind of day it's going to be within the first five minutes after I wake up. I know, because that's when I make the decision. I choose what kind of day it is going to be, and adjust my attitude accordingly. This is something I've learned to do and I'm convinced it is key to managing stress and the day to day tribulations that are part of anyone's life.

Do you start your day by hitting the snooze bar? When the alarm goes off, do you think, "Oh, Gawd, it's morning," and then begin to imagine all the dreary or horrible things that might happen that day? If you do, you may be setting the stage for yourself to have a lousy day. Experts say postponing awakening deprives your brain of the stimuli it needs to churn out mood-elevating hormones, which it typically does within the first five minutes of waking up.

So what you do in the first five minutes of the day are very important. Positive expectations wake the brain, and put you in a better frame of mind. You can help program your day for success as soon as you wake up. How? By thinking of one thing you're looking forward to, or makes you happy.

Pursuing a favorite hobby or whatever makes you feel good — surfing the internet, reading, yoga, painting, having sex, working out, or whatever works for you first thing in the morning — will help you hop out of bed in a pleasant mood. Most importantly, it will set the tone for the rest of your day.

If you face a high-energy day, turn on the tunes to help you get going. Upbeat music increases your heart rate, speeding blood flow to the brain and boosting mood and mental alertness. Good tunes to start the day are ones with a positive, upbeat message.

And if you tend to be an A-type personality, hyper and driven, try Mozart in the morning. Some researchers have evidence that listening to Mozart produces a measurable and positive effect on our brain waves, giving us a smoother and calmer countenance. The result may also be sharper, clearer thinking. Students in a test situation who listened to Mozart prior to writing an exam scored better than those who did not.

The point is to do what works for you. A high powered sales executive might want to "charge him/herself up" in the morning with energetic tunes. Another person may have a nature that is highly reactive, and they could benefit from a calming influence with tranquil, serene music starting their day. We are not all the same. Who hasn't already noticed? We have different lives and therefore will require different decisions. The power comes from knowing ourselves well enough to select what is best for us, and then do it.

I know a very successful creative type who has really learned how to maximize her talents by creating the environment that makes it easier for her to be her best. Her clients are frequently amazed by what she produces, and rightfully so. She's both prolific and effective in her work. How does she do it?

"I learned to do two things well. I learned to manipulate my mood and energy with music, and I learned to manipulate my attitude with self-talk," she says. Plain and simply put.

"Creative work can be extremely draining, and I needed to find ways to conserve my energy and recharge, especially as my career took off and I got busier and busier. I believe that we start each day with a certain number of energy units, and everything we do burns them off. At some point I learned that frenzy burned a lot of energy units, as did other intense emotions," she explains. "I learned to use music to manage my emotions. When I needed to change my attitude I helped myself do it with music and self-talk. I'd tell myself what I needed to hear."

What she has learned to do is something I urge and encourage each and everyone to do. She has learned to be at the controls of her attitude. She calls it manipulating herself because she has realized there are times when how she feels (attitude) is counterproductive to her tasks at hand. She knows she is in control and is responsible for changing it when she must. Her music collection ranges from Mozart to The Tragically Hip. Dire Straits sits next to Ray Charles and Enya. She knows what works for her, and she wastes no time in employing whatever mood-manipulating tactic is musically required. And how does she begin her day?

"Each morning I tell myself that I am the most creative person I know. I tend to be hyperactive, so I modify that with soothing, serene music. I tell myself that what I create that day will be brilliant, effective and the inspiration will come easily. I tell myself that I will be calm, happy, creative and productive. Ever since I started doing that my energy levels remain high, my creativity is boundless and "birthing a concept" has become much easier."

I believe her.

I know because I have experienced the power of harnessing my own attitudes and self-talk. It is amazing what happens when we do. It's powerful stuff.

You can leave your money wallet in your pocket, but you will need to take out your character wallet to become proficient at managing your attitudes and self-talk. Qualities like discipline, determination and belief will be required. They are the "price" to be paid for the power. Isn't it nice to know it is a price everyone can afford?

Plan For A Great Day

Each and every day, I *plan* to have a great day. I *decide* it is going to be great. It is the first decision I make each day.

I start by pumping myself up each morning with high energy tunes. They set the stage for my attitude and outlook. Three times a week I combine this with a good workout. I want to stay in shape to enjoy the many, many more great days I will have the opportunity to plan for in the future.

Music helps me set the stage for my attitude and outlook for the day. Because of this, I choose my selection carefully. I select music not only for the beat, the rhythm and the melody, but for the lyrics. The words are incredibly important to me. It drives my wife nuts, but I can listen to the same song over and over. And over again. If I really like a tune, I'll record it two, or even three times in a row when I make my tapes. Hey, like I say, you must do what works for you!

One of my all time favorites is by the group called America. The song contains a phrase that has stayed with me for years, and sums up my belief system to perfection: *"You can do magic, you can have anything that you desire."*

The New Radicals have a great song (You Get What You Give) that reminds me of a never-give-up-on-your-dreams-or-you-will-die spirit depicted in an old 1980s movie called Flashdance. I love the line, *"We've got the dreamers disease."* I connect with the message that perseverance is the key; to never give up on your dreams. And I use another

86

line "*We only get what we give*," as a constant reminder to give back to society.

I can also highly recommend Gloria Estevan's song called "Reach." It has some terrific words. "*I'll do whatever it takes to follow through with the promise I make and I'll put it all on the line.*" I constantly remind myself with this phrase that it's all about follow through and commitment. Another line in the song is, "*The more I believe all the more this dream will be mine.*" It completely corresponds to one of my favorite affirmations — see it, feel it, believe it and you'll achieve it.

My values are such that my family is incredibly important to me. So Aerosmith's "I Don't Want to Miss a Thing" is a perfect song for me to listen to while visualizing my family together, forever. "*Thank God we are together, I just want to stay with you*," is exactly how I feel about my wife Shawna.

Think about the best that could be!

Train yourself to think of the best possible outcomes to the situations you anticipate facing. Some people automatically go to the worst case scenario, and start their day worrying about what will happen. I suggest that the best thing you could do for yourself is to switch your focus to what could be the most positive outcomes.

Each and every day, I tell myself that I am going to have a great day. As a financial advisor, I would visualize my presentations for the day ahead, and continue the process during my morning shower. In my mind, I would see myself actively listening, and speaking well during my appointments. I would visualize the entire appointment from start to finish in a very positive manner. At the end I would say, "That prospect is going to become a client."

Did it always work out that way? No. But it is an ongoing process. At the end of each successful meeting I would hold a two minute critique with myself and go over what I did well, and what I could improve upon. I used this self-appraisal to my modify my visualizations the next morning.

As time went on I got better and better and better. Did it ever work out 100 percent of the time? No. But I got darn close. In sales lingo, my "closing ratio" ended up at about 95 percent. I'd say that was darn close to all the time.

If you must, fake it until you don't have to anymore.

Do I automatically "feel like it" every day? No, I don't. Some days, quite frankly, I feel exactly the opposite. Thankfully, it is extremely rare, but some days I must really work on that first five minutes of the day. When it is one of those, I remember a phrase to help myself — *Fake it until you make it.* In other words, *pretend* you feel like it. It is possible to alter an attitude by acting as if you already feel that way. I'm told the old Dale Carnegie courses had a similar phrase for these occasions — "ACT enthusiastic and you'll BE enthusiastic."

It's true. If you act enthusiastic long enough, even if you are faking it, you will soon find that you actually feel enthusiastic. Use this principle to your benefit. Pretend you already feel the way you want to feel. Do it long enough and you will find you can stop pretending.

The Enormous Power of Words

Want to change your attitude? Change your words.

Like attitude, our self-talk can empower or debilitate. We can be our own best friend, or our own worst enemy. As usual, the choice is ours to make. Are you a friend or foe to yourself?

During the course of a week, listen to the chatter going on inside your head. How often do you hear yourself say, "I'll never...., or I can't....... or I won't ever........?"

I caution you now, that whatever you are telling yourself — you can't, won't, or will never — will likely be your reality. Our subconscious mind is like a sponge. Whatever we keep telling it will eventually become etched in ourselves and our life experiences.

What we say, especially what we tell ourselves, has an enormous impact on our daily and life experiences. Have you ever started out your day and had a few things go wrong by mid-morning? A colleague or friend phones and asks you how it's going, and you unload, "It's a bad (or other negative description) day!"

You know what? That is about the worst thing you could say because it almost certainly seals your fate to have a bad day. Our words have the power to influence an outcome.

From now on, remember these words: "Up to this point..." Use them to preface a negative statement about your situation. The next time someone asks you how your day is going when it's not going well, instead of saying "I have a headache," or "I'm having a tough day," begin your statement by giving yourself a way out. "Up to this point I've had a headache," and "Up to this point I've had a tough day," allows you the option of change. You have not sentenced yourself to a headache or a 'bad' day for the rest of the day. You have 'opened the door' for change. And you will be surprised at how often things change for you.

There are two halves to the mind — the conscious and the subconscious. The subconscious mind does not have the power of rationality that the conscious mind has. It does not question or judge your input; the subconscious mind merely accepts whatever you say. So your subconscious mind can work for you or against you, depending on what you tell it.

If you keep telling yourself that you can't do something, you won't do it. If you tell yourself you *can* do it, and you tell yourself enough times, the subconscious mind will become a powerful ally and actually help you to achieve it. Quite literally — if you think you can, you are probably right. If you think you can't, you are also likely to be correct.

"While we may not be able to control what happens to us, we can control what happens inside us."

–Benjamin Franklin

Athletic champions have known this for years. Quarterbacks and coaches have said that if there was just one word to describe a successful player, that one word would be attitude. Almost all winning athletes and championship teams are adamant that their attitude and self-talk are the most important ingredients to winning.

"Attitude is a little thing that makes a big difference."
—Author Unknown

An understanding of the magic of attitude does not belong just to athletes. Thomas Jefferson, the third president of the United States had this to say on the subject:

"Nothing can stop the man with the right mental attitude from achieving his goal; nothing on earth can help the man with the wrong mental attitude."

In other words, the negative thoughts we have about our abilities will hold us back from achieving our goals. I couldn't agree more. Carefully chosen words are the best way I know of to control the great force called attitude.

"Think and feel yourself there! To achieve any aim in life, you need to project the end-result. Think of the elation, the satisfaction, the joy! Carrying the ecstatic feeling will bring the desired goal into view."
—Grace Speare

The Case for Precision

*"The difference between the right word and
the almost right word is the difference between
lightning and the lightning bug."*
—Mark Twain

Be careful with the words you use in your self-talk.
Your subconscious (always a receiver of your self-talk) will
take you quite literally. Two words that you probably want
to avoid because they will get you in trouble with any self-
talk are the words 'start' and 'try.' I suggest you remove
the word try from your vocabulary. Don't *try* to do
something. *Do it!*

When you say "Today I am going to start dieting,"
think about what you are saying. The statement insinuates
the initiation of a plan (dieting) but leaves the door open
for an unwanted outcome — that you will merely start.
There is no inference of continuance, or completion. By
the end of the day, you will quite possibly be no longer
dieting.

I am going to start exercising.

I am going to start dieting.

I am going to start being punctual.

I am going to start studying.

I am going to start finding new customers.

I am going to start spending more time with the kids.

I am going to start saving money and investing.

I am going to start doing better.

All of the above statements, and any others that begin with "I am going to start" should be avoided. You are likely to start doing whatever it is, but not have the follow-through or completion. You'll be unhappy and disappointed. Your subconscious will be confused because all it knows is that you got what you said you wanted. You started. If you want to do more than start something, it is best to use a different word.

Will is the Strongest Word of All

The best choice for any self-talk statements, I have learned, is to use the word 'will.' It is a strong word. Notice how the intent of the following sentences is crystal clear.

I will get my RRSP/IRA contribution in early this year.

I will save 10 percent of my income for investing.

I will exercise regularly.

I will study.

I will find new customers for my business.

I will sell more.

I will be punctual.

I will spend more time with my family.

Be as specific as you can when you make your self-talk statements. Your subconscious is always listening, and will endeavor to help you get what you say you want. Exactly as you say it. Make sure you say what you mean, and mean what you say.

Don Cherry played 1,000 pro games, but only one in the NHL. "When I was a boy, I prayed to God to be a pro hockey player. I guess I forgot to say I wanted to be in the NHL," he jokes.

A Tip to Slow Down Time

Want to have more time? We all get just 24 hours a day, but I think we can effect how fast it goes.

If you want to slow down time, tell yourself you have plenty of it. Constantly saying "I have no time" pretty much seals your fate. You will feel as if you never have enough time. You'll try rushing around even faster, and according to Einstein, this will result in time going faster for you.

Instead, tell yourself what you need to hear: "I have plenty of time to do this." or "I'll find the time somehow." It will be far more productive.

A Daily Decision

I believe that each day we can decide what kind of day we are going to have. It starts with a mental decision. This decision can then be enhanced by repeating an affirmation. So the first thing every morning when you wake up, choose one of the following affirmations to say to yourself. Choose the same one every day or mix to match your day.

Think about what you want to improve and start repeating the affirmation aloud to yourself first thing every morning. And repeat it whenever you think of it during the day. Waiting at a traffic light? Repeat the phrase. Long ride in the elevator? Use the time to say it to yourself as many times as you can until you reach your floor. As this starts to become a new habit, you will find plenty of opportunities during the day to use these powerful self-talk messages.

Affirmation #1:

Every day,

in every way,

I am getting better and better.

(The above phrase, or auto-suggestion, was penned by Emile Coué in the 1920's. It is a perfect morning phrase for anyone.)

Affirmation #2:

1. Today I will do more than exist — I will live.

2. Today I will do more than touch — I will feel.

3. Today I will do more than look — I will observe.

4. Today I will do more than read — I will absorb.

5. Today I will do more than hear — I will listen.

6. Today I will do more than listen — I will understand.

7. Today I will do more than think — I will ponder.

8. Today I will do more than talk — I will say something.

(The above words are from John H. Rhodes. They make a great affirmation to develop interpersonal skills and increase the quality of your life.)

Affirmation #3:

(This is my all time favorite.)

Let us become

more than we are,

all that we long to be,

everything we are capable of being.

And then...

Let us long to exceed

what we have become.

—Author Unknown

Affirmation #4:

I See it.

I Feel it.

I believe it.

I will achieve it.

(The above affirmation works well when used in conjunction with your visualizations.)

Chapter 4 Review

- Attitude is a little thing that makes a big difference.

- Faster has become synonymous with better. It isn't true.

- We are in control of our attitude. Always.

- Attitude is power. It levels the playing field.

- Our attitude determines our reaction. Our reaction creates the stress.

- Every decision, every choice has a price or a consequence.

- The first 5 minutes of every day sets our attitude.

- Self-talk can change an unproductive attitude.

- Self-talk influences any outcome.

- Beginning each day with a positive affirmation is extremely beneficial.

Chapter 5

❧

Picking the Big Rocks
in Our Life

Chapter 5

◆

Picking the Big Rocks in Our Life

"We say we don't have enough time. The truth is, every one of us has all the time there is."
—Rachel Orr

When you are young, the future is your currency. Your options are virtually unlimited and everything, and anything, is possible. Youth is the time for broadly dreaming about what you want to do and be. Life is an open highway in front of you. Time is your friend.

That changes. To those who are no longer "young," chronologically speaking, time can become a four-letter word, if you know what I mean.

Middle age, it's been said, is when the broad mind and narrow waist of youth trade places. Time is not as friendly, or kind, as it once seemed. The extent of the hostility, or how much effect the ravages of time have, is entirely up to you. The decisions you make today and the actions you sustain have much to do with your "fitness" as time passes, both physically and financially. Tomorrow never lies.

However, aging seems to be the only way to live a long life. As Keith Richards said, "Getting old is a fascinating thing. The older you get, the older you want to get."

Middle age can be many things, but it is certainly not the time to abandon dreams and goals. Personally, I do not know of an age that does justify an existence without dreams and goals. I plan to live to a proverbial ripe old age, and I intend to have them (dreams and goals) at whatever age that is.

"Youth is a gift of nature, but age is a work of art."
—Garson Klein

Charles Garfield, author of *Peak Performers* (William Morrow & Co.) studied more than 550 top performers and found that, like successful companies, most of them had a mission, or a goal that motivated them to succeed. Happy and successful people apparently have at least one thing in common. They dream their dreams, set their goals and then go about doing the things that will enable them to reach those goals. They determine what is important to

them, what they truly care about, and then d
themselves to that pursuit.

Please reread that last sentence. I suspect it holds
the secret to a happy and fulfilling life. It is so important I
am going to repeat it:

Successful people determine what is important to them, what they truly care about, and then devote themselves to that pursuit.

What successful people do is simple, and something
each and everyone is capable of doing. They establish their
personal priorities and then use those priorities to form
the basis for their actions.

Asking Ourselves the Hard Questions

Is the Jar Full of Rocks?

Years ago I attended a seminar that illustrated the
importance of priorities. This was done with, of all things,
a giant pickle jar. The speaker had set a bunch of big rocks
beside the pickle jar on a table in front of the room. He
placed the big rocks, one by one, inside the jar and when
they reached the top he asked the audience to verify that
the pickle jar was full. Everyone in the audience readily
agreed.

Then he reached down and from under the table took
out a bag of small pebbles and proceeded to pour them
over the big rocks that were already in the "full" pickle jar.
The small pebbles filtered down through the big rocks and
filled up the jar. The speaker then asked the audience the

same question — "Was the jar now full?" We all nodded our heads in agreement. We thought it was fairly obvious that the jar was now full.

The speaker then reached down under the table and brought out a bag of fine sand. He poured the entire bag of fine sand over the small pebbles. It filtered down through the small pebbles and the big rocks and filled the jar. He asked once again, "Is the jar now full?" Most of us once again nodded in agreement, but a few in the audience began to catch on. The speaker smiled and reached under the table one more time.

This time he brought up a pitcher of water. As he poured the water over the fine sand and the small pebbles and the big rocks, it filtered down and eventually filled up the jar. Finally, the jar was completely full. And then he explained...

"The big rocks represent those priorities that matter most. The big rocks are those activities that have the biggest impact on our lives. In a business, the big rocks are the 20 percent of activities that account for 80 percent of the results."

"The problem," he explained, "is that we don't focus on the big rocks. Most of us put the fine sand and the water in first, then the small pebbles. By the time we get to the big rocks — those areas which are most important, that will get us what we ultimately want and account for the biggest part of our success — we just must learn to put the big rocks in first. We must *plan* those activities that get us what we want. They must come first. They are our priorities."

Identifying the 'big rocks' in your life is the first step in getting your life organized. Your big rocks, or your priorities are the foundation of your Life Plan.

What are Your Priorities?

It is absolutely essential for you to determine the priorities in *your* life. What is important to *you*. Forget about what television and magazine ads tell you should be important in your life. Forget about the characters in the shows and movies you watch. Forget about what your friends want, or think they want, or what you think they think they want. That's far too convoluted and anyway, none of that matters. We are, after all talking about *your* life. Your *life*.

Please don't be like some people who spend their entire lives thinking it is someone else's responsibility to make such life decisions for them. No one else is you, so no one else could truly know what is important to you and makes you happy and fulfilled. What makes someone else happy and fulfilled won't necessarily do the same for you.

There is far too much at stake to put some decisions in the hands of others. Personal priorities are definitely in this category. Determining the things that are meaningful to you and make you happy are important decisions. They are your responsibility.

If we don't have clearly defined personal priorities (big rocks), we risk mismanaging our activities. Without knowing it, we can waste years filling our lives with things we enjoy, but have little if any effect on the quality or satisfaction level of our life. We direct all our energy to the sand, pebbles and water in our jar of life. It doesn't matter how much of these you can squeeze into the jar if there is not room left for the priorities or your big rocks. You could end up with a lot of sand, pebbles and water in your life, but have none of the things that truly matter to you.

What do you Value?

Discovering our personal priorities is a soul-searching adventure. If you have never reflected on the subject before, or it has been some time since you last did, it can be quite an eye-opening experience. You might find some surprises.

You may, for example, discover someone else's priorities living in your head. Many of us have accepted extensively marketed concepts that we don't really subscribe to, such as "he who dies with the most toys wins." We may not agree with the concept, but because it has been so frequently suggested in mass media advertising we can begin the act as though we believe it. Without knowing why, we may have placed far too much emphasis on chasing material trinkets. It might take some time, to untangle and separate *your* priorities from those you *thought* were yours.

Here are some questions to ask yourself:

- What do I cherish, admire, prize or treasure?

- What do I think, feel and believe are good, desirable or important?

- What are the qualities I wish to have in my life?

108

- What qualities do I want to pass on to my children?

- What do I want to be known for?

- What do I value?

- If I knew I only had one year left to live, what would be important to me?

Think long and hard about your answers to these questions. They indicate your values and are key to uncovering your personal priorities. Because if our values don't flat out determine our priorities, they are certainly linked to them.

For example, if you value independence, having a solid financial plan that protects your independence through your retirement years should be a priority for you. But it will be a priority only if you recognize and acknowledge the value you place on independence, and the freedom of having choices. Want to know if it's important to you? Just imagine life without it. Sometimes it takes imaging what it would be like *without* something for us to realize just how important it is to us.

Personal priorities vary from individual to individual. Some folks value being able to make a difference. Yesterday I read in the newspaper about an anonymous donor who gifted a school breakfast program on the brink of closure due to lack of funding. Because of his or her generosity (his or her values) a substantial number of children who otherwise wouldn't have breakfast, will. They will be better nourished, and from what I've heard about the importance of eating a good breakfast, these kids will also learn better. This breakfast program made a big difference to them.

If you value the ability to make a difference, putting money aside to do so will be a priority of yours. Perhaps you'd like to be able to help your son or daughter get started in their own business, or you'd feel really good about being able to help educate the grandchildren you know one day you'll have. If you truly want to be able to do these things, then you should plan your life so that you will be able to do them. My experience is that if you don't plan for something, it rarely happens the way you want.

What do you value?

As you think about this, here are some trigger words that maybe helpful to the process:

loyalty, relationships, honesty, freedom, courage, family, diligence, determination, fairness, commitment, humor, love, helping others, fitness, spirituality, growth, health, peace of mind, knowledge, leadership, patience, friendships, time for ourselves, time for others, education, security, organization, reliability, compassion, and responsibility.

The words listed above are given as prompts or ideas for you. Obviously, it is impossible to list all possible values. There are no right or wrong answers; the point is to come up with a list of the values that are meaningful to *you*.

One other tip — Go for the ideals. Aim high! If there is ever an appropriate place for ideals in the real world, this is it. In fact, that is precisely what it is all about. We want to be able to identify those qualities we respect and admire, and to which we aspire.

Is Money that Important?

Some of you may have noted that in the value possibilities list above, I made no mention of sail boats, sleek cars, designer labels, or any other material niceties. That's because rarely is money the 'big rocks' in someone's life.

We may think that money is the most important thing, but chasing money for money's sake can soon feel like an empty existence. Yes, we all need money. But without an attachment to one of our personal values, the pursuit of money can be meaningless. The 'why' of money must be answered with something that is personal and meaningful to us.

Let's say, for example, that you are an average person who knows you should be putting money away and investing for the future. We all know about compound interest (if you don't, reread *The Wealthy Barber*, and if you have never read *The Wealthy Barber*... where have you been?!) We all know that the sooner we start the better. We all know that we should be saving 10 to 20 percent of our income, depending on our current age. We all know this. But apparently few of us are actually doing it, as was discussed in a previous chapter.

I think the reason so many people aren't doing it is because they have never solidly linked the priority (saving money) with a personal value (such as independence, security, comfort, or philanthropic natures). I think that unless the link between our priorities and values is clearly established and kept in our hearts and minds, we will inevitably lose our focus.

We may start out with firm intentions to invest 10 percent of our income, for example. We start doing it because we know we should. But if it isn't crystal clear to us *why* we should, for reasons that matter to *us* and are based on our personal values, we won't do it for long. We'll stop, and blame it on a lack of discipline.

I've got some news for you: we are already as disciplined as we are ever going to get. Forget about thinking that all you need is more discipline. It is unlikely that is your problem anyway.

Usually it's our habits that cause all the trouble. So if our habits are not in line with our priorities and values, we need to know. We usually will. We will know that something is amiss, but we may not be able to put our finger on it.

It reminds me of a lady I'll call Carolyn. She sunk into her chair one day and in an almost hopeless voice remarked on how she felt like she was just spinning her wheels. She was exhausted from her job, and the long commute to and from work each day. The fact that she had so little time to be with her children made her feel worse. She held a good job, her husband did too, but it didn't seem to matter how much money they made they lived from payday to payday. She was frustrated and often short-tempered.

"We want to be saving and investing, we know we should, but where is the money going to come from?" she despaired.

When Carolyn took the time to examine and compare her priorities, values and habits she found her answers. She listed her monthly expenses and they looked something like this:

- Car lease payment $500.00

- Clothes $400.00

- Restaurants..$350.00

- Laundry & Dry cleaning $130.00

- Home Cleaning Service $240.00

Then she compared them with her 'big rocks' or priorities and her personal values. In those categories she'd written the following list:

- Independence.

- Knowledge and education.

- A good marriage.

- A strong family unit.

- Time with her children.

- A comfortable retirement with her husband.

When Carolyn compared the two lists, she could see that her habits were not in line with her priorities and personal values. They did not match. She was spending a large portion of her money each month on things that had nothing to do with what she valued. It was no wonder she felt discouraged and frustrated.

Happily, Carolyn was a proactive kind of gal. She remade a number of her decisions. She came to decide that she didn't need such an expensive car, she cut her clothes budget in half, kept the laundry and dry cleaning expense, and whittled down the restaurant and home cleaning expenses. She wavered on the restaurant and home cleaning service, but realized that cooking at home would give her the opportunity to spend more time with her husband and children (which she identified as a priority and value). The result was that Carolyn found the money that she needed for saving and investing. It had always been there, but her habits were incongruent with her goals.

Mismatched habits and priorities usually result in a lack of something somewhere in our lives. Lack of satisfaction. Lack of motivation. Unfulfilled desires. About the only place that mismatched habits and priorities will result in abundance is around the waist line!

Many people who have succeeded in losing unwanted weight credit a new alignment of their habits and priorities as the cause of their success. They say it wasn't the diet, per se, it was the new habits aligned with their ideals.

Makes sense to me. If we value health and desire a trim figure, losing weight will become one of our 'big rocks.' Habits such as overeating, eating the wrong foods, or inactivity (sofa-surfing) are incongruent with the priority of losing weight. All the discipline in the world won't do a darn thing unless the habits are changed.

If, when you finalize your list of personal priorities and values, you notice that some of your habits are incongruent, accept this information with a positive frame of mind. Knowing what's causing the trouble is the first step to fixing it. And the good news is that habits can always be changed. We formed them in the first place, so we can always decide to form new ones. New habits are easier to form when we are motivated. Staying in touch with our Personal Priorities and Values (the reason for our change in behavior) can provide the motivation.

The Write Stuff

Whatever is important to you must be recognized and acknowledged by you. That's the first step. The next step is to write it down. A phrase I learned years ago — *Think it and ink it!* — became one of my personal habits for a very compelling reason.

I made it a habit to write things out because writing things out is incredibly powerful. The simple act of writing it down on a piece of paper, and signing it, strongly increases the likelihood of its occurrence.

I don't know why this works so well, but it does. Many theories have been proposed, and most speculate that it relates to messages received by our subconscious. The theories are all very interesting, but you know what? *Why* it works doesn't matter. I just know that *it does work.*

I don't need to know how my computer works, either. What matters is that I have learned which keys and commands produce the desired results. *How* it works is unimportant; *that* it works is what matters.

" Absence of evidence is not evidence of its absence."
—Anonymous

The Write Sign

After I have written out what I believe or wish to achieve, I always date and sign it. Somehow this formalizes my agreements with myself and crystallizes my serious intent. I am giving my word, or my oath to myself. This is also in the category of "I-don't-know-why-this-works-but-it-does," and I highly recommend you sign your writings too.

Writing it out is also a way to keep focused. After you have composed a list of your values, or principles, don't let that piece of paper get lost in a desk drawer. It won't do you any good if it is hidden from view. Keep it where you can refer to it often.

I found that if I kept referring frequently to what I had written, I stayed motivated to form the habits that would help me achieve my goals. They were goals that I very much wanted to achieve, and I had mapped out the activities that I knew I had to do, each day, to achieve them. By keeping them forefront in my mind, I knew what I had to do, and who I had to be each day. I became more and more focused and determined as I began to see myself forming new habits. Over time, I was able to turn my ideals into my realities. You can too!

A conviction in the power of the written word is shared by my wife, Shawna. In fact, after we compiled a list of our values and priorities, we had them wordsmithed and our "Gordon Family Philosophy" hangs in our home where we see it each and every day. We never forget who we are, and what we believe and value.

The Gordon Family Philosophy

We are The Gordon Family.

Our home is a haven for Honesty, Friendship, Love and Respect. It is a safe platform for each of us to learn, to change and to grow. We aspire to become all we can be, and then do more. We are gentle with ourselves, and each other.

We share and enjoy our passion, and endless zest for life. Our commitment to each other is solid and trusted. We focus on our goals, while ever mindful that life is a journey not destination. We are a team, and will always be humble and grateful for what we have created together.

Each day we will live by our principles, and those we have come to value: Loyalty, Diligence, Courage, Fairness and Responsibility. We make these choices willingly, happily and lovingly. We look forward to our future because of the choices we make today.

We, The Gordon Family, love each other.

We, The Gordon Family, love that

tomorrow never lies.

✦

Chapter 5 Review

- We say we don't have enough time, but the truth is that each of us has all the time there is.

- Successful people determine what is important to them, what they truly care about and then devote themselves to that pursuit.

- It is our responsibility to figure out our own priorities and values.

- We must put our big rocks (priorities) in the jar of life first.

- Our priorities should form the basis for our actions.

- Mismatched priorities will result in a lack or longing somewhere in our lives.

- We need to get clear about what we want and value, write it down and sign it.

What do you stand for?

What kind of person (family) do you want to be?

Chapter 6

❦

Bound by a Binder
It's a Family Affair

Chapter 6

Bound by a Binder
It's a Family Affair

"We are, each of us, angels with only one wing and we can only fly by embracing each other."

—Luciano de Crescenzo

There's no doubt in my mind that the best financial plan you could ever have is to stay married to your soul mate, and to have a sound financial *and* Life Plan with her/him. It's so much easier with two! Over the long term, it is so much better in so many ways if you stay together.

On this point, I'd like to share a joke with you that made its way to me. It goes something like this —

A fellow went into the toy store to select a present for his daughter's birthday. She'd made a request for a Barbie doll, so the fellow asked the store clerk to show him what was available.

"Gladly, sir," the clerk responded. "Over here, we have Veterinary Barbie, School Teacher Barbie and Stockbroker Barbie," he said as he led the fellow over to the Barbie doll section.

"How much?" the fellow inquired as he examined the little outfits and paraphernalia that depicted the occupation in each package.

"Each of those goes for $19.95," the clerk informed him. "We also have Astronaut Barbie, Accountant Barbie and Movie Star Barbie for the same price. And over here we have a real special Barbie. She goes for $75 dollars," he continued and reached for one to show the fellow.

"Seventy-five dollars!" the fellow exclaimed. "Whatever makes her so expensive?"

"Well," explained the clerk, "she's called Divorce Barbie. She comes with a house and a car!"

That joke hits a point of understanding with just about everyone over the age of consent today. I doubt very much if it would have made the rounds in offices during the 1950s. Back then, there would not have been that point of common understanding, and the joke would have bombed. Divorce was uncommon, and talked about in whispers. The divorce rate then reflected the common attitude, which was different than it is today.

Oh boy, is it ever different today!

Nearly 35 percent of marriages in Canada end in divorce court, and the number is even higher in the United States(56 %). That means at least one in three walks down the aisle end unhappily. Most of us marry at least twice. But, increasingly, many of those marriages tank as well, and third marriages are becoming more and more common.

The result has been a change in "family life cycles," according to a StatsCan document, *Canadian Families at the Approach of the Year 2000*. Gone are the days of wedding-chapel-to-baby's-crib-to-kid's-college-graduation cycle. It has been replaced with what authors Yves Peron and Evelyne Lapierre-Adamcyk have labeled "the family life courses of individuals." Which, simply put, means that many people will live inside a number of family structures. We live within our own nuclear family for a while, then maybe in a single-person household with joint-custody arrangements for another bit of time, and finally perhaps in a "blended family," where the children are an artful combo of mine, yours and ours.

Why is marriage in such a forlorn state?

There are many theories proposed, but one worth pondering is Los Angeles author Marion F. Solomon's "take" on love and marriage in her book *Narcissism and Intimacy: Love and Marriage in the Age of Confusion*. Ms. Solomon, a UCLA professor, believes she knows the identity of the culprit undermining modern marriages.

According to Ms. Solomon, the culprit is called rampant, pathological self-absorption. Ouch! Sounds like a Boomer's life!

Whatever theory is correct, the impact of divorces on our families is significant. It's confusing for everyone. And it is ubiquitous. In a sixth grade class of my friend's daughter, Olivia, the teacher asked who had their original parents. In other words, who had the same mom and the same dad to which they were born. Only five hands went up in a class of nearly 30 students.

It makes me wonder just how funny the Barbie doll joke really is, if you think about it.

I can't help but think about all the women who are divorced and *don't* come with a house and a car. And what about the men who are doggedly trying to build a new life with their new families on what is left over each month after paying the alimony, maintenance and child support payments from their previous relationship(s)?

The High Price of Divorce

It may not just be the Boomers unrestrained spending habits that have caused them to be in such poor financial shape as a generation. (I am referring, of course, to reports of their negative, or record low savings.) Another contributing factor that has put them behind the financial Eight Ball has undoubtedly been their divorces. Because the financial consequences of divorce are very high.

Every time there is a marital split, both parties lose financial ground. Even if the assets are split fairly, equitably and even amicably, both parties pay a high price. The home is sold and both husband and wife re-enter the real estate market looking for housing to replace their marital home. Because they only have half the money, they can only look at half the house. They learn a new meaning for the word downsizing, and hopefully the market hasn't compounded the situation with much higher prices than when the marital home was purchased. Unfortunately, it often does.

Any accumulated savings and investments are also split or sold. Often, the timing is poor. And any compounding effect on their savings is disrupted, as each partner once again begins at square one. Frequently money that previously went to savings and investments now goes to replace material possessions, soothe injured egos or simply make ends meet.

And that is just adding up some of the obvious financial prices. The emotional price can be, and often is, very high. Divorce can really take the wind out of your sails, and capacities can be reduced by depression and sadness for quite a while. And extra costs are often incurred for counseling as the spouses and the children learn to cope with the life changes.

Any way you look at it, divorce is devastating.

Unless, of course you buy into that philosophy that purports "The best financial plan you could ever have is that the last check (cheque, for Canadian readers) you ever write bounces." According to the author of this philosophy, you should spend it all while you are alive and to heck with anyone else, family or not. This is perfect if you want to make marriage and divorce your hobby. Because with a succession of divorces, there is a high probability that money will be a stranger to your bank account. Just ask former tennis pro Vic Seixas.

Fifty trophies fill the china cabinet in the tiny apartment where Vic lives alone. The most prestigious is the one inscribed "singlehanded championship of the world" that he won in Wimbledon in 1953. He is now 76 and supports himself with two bartending jobs.

Even though Vic played tennis during a time when trophies, not checks, were the reward for winning, he made some decent money as a stockbroker for 17 years in Philadelphia. But then there were his divorces.

Half of what he had went to his first wife more than 20 years ago, and half of what was left of that went to his second wife. That left Vic Seixas with a quarter, and he still had to pay child support for his only daughter, now a 19-year-old college sophomore.

Although many in a similar situation feel bitterness, Vic doesn't. He is too busy working.

"People ask, 'Why are you bartending at this age?' I like to eat," Vic says with a laugh.

In my mind there is no question about it: **The best Financial Plan is to stay married and have a Life Plan with your mate.**

"A good marriage resembles a pair of shears, so joined that they cannot be separated; often moving in opposite directions, yet always punishing anyone who comes between them."

—Sidney Smith

Bring Your Values and Dreams Together. Forever!

I make no claims to be a marriage counselor or therapist, but I have some theories as to why marriages don't hold together. And what might keep them together.

It hinges on the partners *believing* they will be together for life. Almost all marriages start out that way. But somehow, somewhere along the way, this is forgotten. "We" stops being part of the thinking and the vocabulary. It is replaced with "I" and "you." Soon, the couple forgets that they are in it together, that they are a team, a "we."

Many well-meaning experts and professionals unwittingly help couples forget about the "we" in their relationships. For years, magazines with a female readership have been pointing out to their market that women *should* establish separate financial arrangements. Have your own checking account! Make sure you have your own savings account! And lots of professional heads have nodded in agreement. Listen to this story a golf buddy told me...

For quite a while he'd been hearing good things about a certain accountant, and had finally decided to check him out. He made an appointment. A few days later after reviewing my buddy's financial affairs, the accountant called him back in for a discussion. He said that by and large, everything seemed fine but he was very concerned about something he said was missing. My friend's conversation with him went something like this at their second meeting:

"Like I said, everything is in pretty good shape, but I'm very concerned about something that is missing. Tell me, have you thought about establishing a Personal Protection Account?" the accountant asked my buddy.

"Huh?"

"A Personal Protection account. They are usually set up in an off-shore account, and the only people who have to know about it are you and me," the accountant offered.

"You mean my wife wouldn't know about it?" my friend asked, beginning to catch on.

"Yeah, of course not. That's the whole point!"

It didn't even occur to the accountant that my buddy might not be in total, one hundred percent agreement with him on this concept. (He wasn't. Not at all.)

I know where my friend is coming from.

I am not in agreement with a "what's mine is mine, and what's yours is yours" philosophy any more than I agree with another attitude I sometimes encounter. The one that seems to be a "what is mine is mine and what is yours is mine too!" These attitudes, in my opinion, drive a wedge in a couple's commitment. This is *not* a good thing, in Martha Stewart language.

Yet I find these attitudes shockingly common among couples. Each wants their own bank accounts, their own money, their own investments and the often argue about whose turn it is to pay for what. The lines are drawn in the sand, and although formalized as a couple, each party figuratively remains on their own side of the lines.

*"Blessed is the couple who believe in multiplying,
rather than dividing."*

—Anonymous

I have clients who are classic examples of this. Take Mr. and Mrs. Rueleaux, for example. They have been married 30 years, during which each had professional careers. She had been a successful corporate video producer and he had a respected millworking shop. Because of a disability, Mr. Rueleaux had to quit working at age 50. Nonetheless, they have half a million dollars placed with me, and they had come to see me for their annual financial check-up.

Thanks to computer technology, I have the capability to link all family investments together. In preparation for their appointment, I had done exactly that for them. We would still view his and her portfolios separately, but I thought they might be interested in first seeing how they were doing "together."

I was wrong.

Almost immediately, I could tell that Mrs. Rueleaux didn't like it one little bit. "Mrs. Rueleaux, I can see from your body language that you aren't comfortable with this," I said.

"Well, I don't like it," she quickly responded. "Why don't you report the accounts separately?"

I attempted to explain to her that we could still do that, but that it might be interesting to see how their "Family Investment Corporation" was doing. I didn't get far.

"This is MY money," she hotly stipulated. "If and when I die, it's HIS money. But right now it's MY money. His money is HIS money. My money is MY money."

I really don't understand this kind of thinking, and I am at a loss trying to comprehend the attitude. The only thing worse is when couples have separate portfolios and do not share information with each other, resulting in duplications of their investments.

Call me old-fashioned if you like, but I believe in "we" and "ours." That's what marriage is all about — togetherness. And commitment is forever. We all start out that way on our wedding day. It really is best if we keep it that way. For many reasons, not the least of which is financial.

Note to Single Persons:

The following material will work for you just as well even if you don't currently have a partner. When you do meet your soul mate, you'll be ready with Life Plan skills that you can teach and integrate into your relationship with your partner. Maybe they'll have read this book too, and then the two of you can combine Life Plans.

B is for Binder.

In 1983 I bought a simple, large, 3-ringed black binder. I still have it. That simple black binder was, perhaps, one of the wisest purchases I ever made. Not because it's a binder, but because of what it has been used for, and the difference it has made in my life. If 'A' is for Attitude, then 'B' is for Binder.

I was in the beginning stages of my career in the financial industry when I bought it. I was full of dreams and visions for my future, and I was committed to becoming the best at my job that I could. I wanted to be one of the best that ever was, just like when I was a kid playing hockey and dreaming of becoming the next Bobby Orr.

My life wasn't perfect (whose is?) and I had set some personal goals to achieve, in addition to my career goals. I longed for my Ms. Right, my soul mate with whom to have a family. I'd embarked on a dedicated search, but had not yet met her. I also had my eye on a few material possessions and a lifestyle I wanted to acquire. Having grown up in a house with no shower, I had determined long ago that one day I'd live in a wonderful house, drive my ideal car and raise the perfect family with a beautiful wife. I also wanted to run a marathon

I began collecting images and pictures that represented the goals I wished to attain — a beautiful woman, my ideal car, the style of home I wanted and photos of successful men I chose as role models. I was serious about the marathon and found a picture depicting the perfect male running body and pasted a photo of my own face over top. I took all my clipped images from magazines, ad layouts and newspapers and organized them in my binder, along with my written goals.

I believed they would all happen for me. But I didn't expect any of them to land in my lap without effort. I worked hard at developing good habits that would bring me closer to my goals, both personal and career-wise. At work each day, I made sure I went the extra mile to meet, or exceed, my target for the day and give the best possible service to my clients. Using the discipline I learned in athletics, I cut myself very little slack. But I didn't mind. I was determined to reach my goals. I designed a training program to be physically in shape for the marathon, and I religiously stuck to it.

At first, I operated on sheer faith, hanging on to a group of words I'd picked up at a seminar: "If you can conceive it, and you believe it, you *can* achieve it!"

Those words rang through my mind over and over and over. I wrote them out on a page and inserted them into my black binder. I memorized them. More accurately, I etched them forever in my mind. Occasionally, I caught myself saying them to myself, over and over and over. I liked those words. More importantly, I believed those words.

If you can conceive it,

and you believe it,

you can achieve it!

One of the first goals written in my binder that I achieved was running a marathon. I will always remember that day. It was the one and only marathon I ever ran, although fitness remains a personal priority with me. But that day was a defining moment in my life.

Success comes to every size, style and shape of determination.

There were so many different shapes of bodies and running styles among the marathon participants! Some looked as though they couldn't possibly run a block, never mind a marathon. Yet they came in under three hours. Others, who looked fit as a fiddle, dropped to the sidelines early. Success comes to every size, style and shape of determination.

Personal triumph was mine that day. Not only did I finish the marathon, but I did so in a very respectable time. My sense of accomplishment was enormous, and it fueled my fires regarding my other goals. I continued to work even harder, kept focused on my goals and my belief that I could achieve them.

My quest for self-education continued and I was an eager participant in numerous courses and seminars offered within my industry. I was an enthusiastic student, always ready to learn from others who were willing to share their secrets of success. Needless to say, I met some interesting and dynamic people.

"Behold the turtle. He makes progress only when he sticks his neck out."

—James Bryant Conant

Visualize for Added Power

It was at one of the many seminars and courses I attended that I was introduced to the power of visualization. If you haven't yet discovered this technique, let me share with you its magic.

I call it magic because no one can explain exactly how it scientifically works. I am not bothered by the lack of scientific explanation. I have used it and I know it works. I don't need to know how something works before I use it. If I needed to know how things worked before I used them, I would never have a bill for electricity. Nor would I enjoy the benefits of it.

In a way, learning the art of visualization was an expansion of the type of dreaming I did as a kid. My childhood hockey-hero dreams helped develop my ability to imagine. And that is a key to visualization — the ability to vividly imagine. No other special skills are required. Everyone can do this!

Visualization is really quite simple. To begin with, get in a quiet place and clear your mind as best you can. Then, clearly imagine the goal you wish to attain. Imagine it in every minute detail. How will you feel when you achieve it? What will you say? Where will you be? Who will you be with? What will you be doing? See it happen. Feel it happening. Hear your delight and the pleasure of those with whom you share it. Smile. Feel the warm glow of satisfaction. The more detail you can conjure, the more effective your visualization will be.

That's about all there is to it, except that you should do it regularly. Take a few moments every day, if you can, and repeat the visualization process with your goals. Remember the details. Engage as many of the senses — sight, sound, touch, smell — in your visualizations as you can. At the very least, do this weekly.

You are the Movie Director!

The best part of visualization is that you are the director of your own movie. Think of yourself as the director and your visualization as the movie. You are the one in control and calling all the shots. Make the movie exactly as you want it to be. Have everyone in it say exactly what you want them to say and do exactly according to your wishes. As you can imagine, this can be a very enjoyable process.

You might be surprised how effective this technique is for setting the tone for the day. Any day. Want to have a great day? In the morning, visualize the perfect day. See, hear and feel everything happening just how you want it. By doing so, you will increase the likelihood of its occurrence.

Professional sales people or business owners facing a day with a full round of meetings would do well to use this technique. Instead of concentrating on what might go wrong (after all, you are thoroughly prepared, right?) concentrate on what will go right. Visualize your meetings going well. Extremely well. Hear yourself saying precisely the right things. See your clients happily agreeing to your proposal. Feel the satisfaction of 'winning.' As always, do this in a much detail as you can.

Years ago, I developed and added these new visualization skills to my repertoire. Not only did I continue to write, sign and regularly read my goals, I began to visualize them happening. In my mind I could see them happening. I could hear, smell and feel them happening.

"Scientific management and computers
will never reduce the importance
of the effective dreamer."
—Herman C. Krannert

Sharing Your Dreams with the Right People

I was in my twenties when I began signing my letters "Positively, Ken Gordon." I also stopped using the word 'try' and it was about the same time that I began believing that anything, and everything was possible. I figured there was no reason in the world *not* to aim for the stars. Maybe I wouldn't reach them, but I'd sure as heck hit the moon. Yes, my goals were lofty. And yes, it made a few people nervous.

"If a man does not keep pace with his companions,
perhaps it is because he hears a different drummer.
Let him step to the music which he hears,
however measured or far away."
—Henry David Thoreau

The first people to glimpse the newly focused and positive Ken Gordon were, of course, my immediate family. They were the first to experience the changes in my language and attitude. My parents and siblings would listen to me proclaim my goals and direction, and they would shake their heads. I don't know whether or not it made them nervous, but I do know that at first they attributed my new language and beliefs in myself to something akin to brainwashing. They waited for it to pass, and for me to return to normal. In the meantime, my mother clipped the Careers & Opportunities section from the newspapers and taped them to my bedroom door.

"Mom, you can't rush the great ones," I would say, still fixed on my dreams and goals.

I found it was very helpful to arrange times to be with "like-minded" people, such as my friend Alex. I've known Alex for years and we still meet for lunch once a month. I share my deepest dreams. He listens. He encourages. He cheers me on. And he shares his deepest dreams and goals with me. We exchange tips and insights. Best of all, we believe in each other, and we believe in tomorrow. As he said in a recent email, "There is no price too high to pay for one to follow his dreams."

I do not have that kind of relationship with all my friends. Some of my friends have a "live for the moment" lifestyle. Dreams, goals, visualizations and self-talk affirmations are not such a big part of their world. And that's fine. That's what makes them who they are. People are different. As such, we bring different things to relationships, and share different things.

As I shared my goals with friends and family, I found that reactions went either of two ways. People were either supportive, or they weren't. I learned to share my dreams with the people who could help me by being supportive. I decided I was in control, it was my life, and I would not let what anyone else thought shake me off the path I was on.

Naysayers have never been my favorite people. You know the kind of people I mean — whatever you say you want to do, they are the first ones to tell you 150 (or more) reasons why it won't work. Or why it isn't a good idea. Or what will go wrong. Or who already tried that and failed.

I have two words of advice for you regarding naysayers: *avoid them*. And if *you* are a naysayer, prone to immediately point out the negative, I have one word for you: *stop*. Despite how passionately you may believe we need to hear what you have to say, we don't. You can be of great assistance to us by keeping your negative thoughts and comments to yourself. Please. And thank you.

Even though there were times when I felt as though I was swimming against the current, I stuck to my guns and my detailed plans and goals. Yes, I worked hard. But over time, every one of my goals were met. Every single one.

Some were even exceeded. I rose to the top in my field and earned the respect of my colleagues and the loyalty of my clients. I met the lady of my dreams and won her heart. My Binder became Our Binder. Together we have three precious children, live in our beautiful mortgage-free home, and continue to dream and be excited about our future.

Never stop believing in yourself and your dreams, even if you have no one to share them with. Hone your self-talk, and practice your visualizations. Stay focused and determined and you will get there. If I can do it, so can you.

*"Some people see things as they are and ask why.
I dream dreams that never were and ask why not."*

—George Bernard Shaw

Your Children are Watching

*"Live so that when your children think of caring,
fairness and integrity, they think of you."*

–Anonymous

Let's face it, our children learn from us no matter what we do. A close friend who has also achieved extraordinary levels of success, says his own father was his inspiration. But not because he was particularly *good* at being a father and husband, but because he was *so bad* at it.

My friend grew up watching his father drink a bottle of rye every day while smoking his brains out. He was everyone's friend (he loved to drink) but privately he often whined about how poorly life treated him. He never planned for his future and when he reached retirement, he was in dire financial shape, and felt helpless to do anything about it. From his father, my friend learned what *not* to do.

141

My friend vowed to be different kind of person and father to his own children. To this day he has kept his word.

I want my children to grow up and become happy, productive members of our global community because of me, not in spite of me. I don't ever want my kids to think of me in the way my friend thinks of his father.

I know my children are watching. Just how closely children watch us and follow our example hit close to home recently while I was reviewing one of the chapters for this book.

I work out in the mornings, and use this time even more efficiently by seizing the opportunity to catch up on my reading. On this particular morning, it was a new chapter fresh from Rachel's computer. I was reading it when I saw my three-year old son, Chase come downstairs into my workout room.

Chase looked at me and took it all in. Then took his little shirt off (as I had done earlier) and began to make his way to the stairmaster when he changed course for no apparent reason and went back upstairs. I didn't think anything more of it until a few minutes later when Chase returned.

He'd gone upstairs to get a magazine which he was now solemnly and deliberately placing it for "reading" while he was "exercising," just like his dad was doing. The magazine might have even been upside down, which in itself didn't matter because Chase hasn't yet learned how to read! He was just doing what his dad was doing! At that moment, I could not have been more proud of being a father.

Bind with a Binder

*"Before anything else, getting
ready is the secret to success."*
—Henry Ford

I recommend the following to anyone who will take my advice:

1. Go out and get yourself a big binder.

2. Create the following sections in it—

    * Our Family Philosophy

    * Our Written Goals (mental, physical, emotional and spiritual).

    * Our relationship goals.

    * Financial Plan

    * Retirement Projections

    * Registered Plan Records (IRA/RRSP, RRIF, RESP)

    * Financial Cash Account Statements & Records

    * Loan & Liabilities — Mortgage Amortization Schedule

    * Tax Documents

    * Insurance Policies & Health Coverage

- Will/Power of Attorney

- Dare to Dream

3. Begin writing down your dreams and goals for each section. Ask your spouse to do the same, but do not show each other your lists. At least, not yet...

4. Begin collecting images from magazines, newspapers, calendars, greeting cards, posters, etc. that represent your goals.

5. Memorize the following words: Whatever my mind can conceive and believe, I can achieve.

For more information, visit our website at:

www.tomorrowneverlies.com

Chapter 6 — Review

- The best financial plan ever is to stay married and have a good financial and Life Plan with our mate.

- Divorce costs. A lot. In lots of ways.

- Strong, long term relationships are built with "we" thinking and acting.

- If we can conceive it, and we solidly believe it, we can achieve it.

- Visualization works like magic if we practice it.

- Our children are watching. Our habits are our legacy to our children.

- It is time to begin getting my/our Binder together.

Chapter Seven

P
O
P-O-W-E-R
E
R

Chapter Seven

P

O

P-O-W-E-R

E

R

*O*f you look up the word power in the dictionary, it is described as "the capacity or ability to do or accomplish something." According to Mr. Webster, if we have the ability or wherewithall to do something, we have power. We have power! We have the power to do and be whatever is within our capability.

The question is what we will do with the power. Will we do nothing with it, and allow it to remain idle in a state of pure potential? Or will we take the bull by the horns, so to speak, and turn that potential into something tangible?

Remember, you have the power. A Life Plan gives you turbo power.

Your **P**lan for Life is an **O**ngoing process of "We-thinking" and acting. Enjoy the journey, **R**eward yourself wisely, and you'll experience real family **P-O-W-E-R.**

Plan for Life is an

On going process of

We-thinking and acting.

Enjoy the journey, and

Reward yourself wisely.

Plan for Life

Someone once said that without a plan, you are planning to fail. I think whoever said that was right. A Plan for Life means exactly that — a plan for your life. A plan for how you want to experience your time on this planet.

This is really important stuff.

Other than the instinct to protect the life of your child, the desire to live is the strongest known human impulse. We all have a very strong instinct to survive. But as human beings we want to do more than survive, and it is natural to desire more than merely an existence. We all want to enjoy our time here. We want to be happy.

When our forefathers drafted The American Charter of Rights, they recognized this important universal desire for happiness. The Charter clearly states and protects a "right to pursue happiness."

It is our right and it is also our responsibility. Please note that it does not say "we have a right to happiness." It says we have a right to *pursue* happiness. This requires action. Many people make the mistake of thinking that happiness should come to them and they passively spend their entire lives waiting for it to happen. It rarely, if ever, does. So they spend the rest of their lives bitterly complaining, as if they were short-shrifted.

Your Plan for Life is your plan for happiness. You must choose and commit to the actions that will be the life and lifestyle *you* ultimately want to live. What makes you happy? Get your Binder out and turn to the section where you have recorded your Family Philosophy. The life you choose should be a true reflection of *your* written Family Philosophy, and vice versa. Your written Family Philosophy should also be a reflection of your actions.

Always remember that your life is not about what other people want or do. It is about what you and your family want or do. Forget about keeping up with "The Jones." Trust me when I tell you: The Joneses don't care. Not one iota!

Assessing Your Situation

Remember in the last chapter when I asked you and your partner to write out your goals and priorities individually? Well, it's time now to sit down and look at each other's lists.

When some couples do this, they find themselves reading a list of goals and priorities that bear striking resemblance to their own list. Although worded slightly differently, each partner has goals and objectives similar to the other. This is not always the case, so you might want to brace yourself for some surprises before you read your partner's list!

Many couples find different items on each other's lists. I want to point out that differences are okay. They can even be good because one of you may have written down a desire that the partner has overlooked that is also important to her/him. The items that are different are not to be tossed out or eliminated. If they are important, they are to be worked in to the Life Plan.

Get together and talk about each other's lists. The objective is not for one party to convince the other that his list is better than hers or hers is more important than his. What is important is that the two of you not get into a tug-of-war over which part of the Life Plan gets top priority — mortgage pay down, IRAs or RRSPs, Investment Accounts or a vacation. What you want to do is reach a consensus. You must both agree on the priority of each item that is entered in the Family Binder as an 'official' goal.

Of course, the more goals that you both share, the easier it will be to accomplish this phase of your Family Binder or Life Plan. But when there are differences, and this is often the case, it usually takes significant dialogue between the partners to work it out to where both are comfortable. There is no right or wrong; what is right for you is right for you. Please take as long as it takes to reach the necessary consensus. This plan does not work unless you are both aligned in the same direction and 'singing off the same song sheet.'

Short, Medium and Long-Term Goals

At the end of each fiscal year, many companies hold meetings to determine the goals they would like the organization to achieve over a three to five year time span. Couples can use the same technique to give their lives and their Life Plan direction. Ask yourselves: Do we want to buy a new home? Change careers or jobs? Upgrade our education by going back to school? Have more time with the family? Pursue new hobbies? Grow the RRSP or IRA account? Consider what you are satisfied with, and what you would like to change. Then decide whether it is something you want to put into place immediately, within a few years or if it is something that will be accomplished over a longer range of time.

The Big Question

Do I have (or will I have) enough money to retire is usually the #1 Question. It is a tough question. But it is one that you must answer yourself. In my profession, many couples have asked me when I think they should retire and how much I think they need to accumulate prior to retirement. It has always been my position that it is their decision to make. Not mine. I can help them figure it out, but there is no magic formula because everybody's magical nut is different. Besides, why would you defer such an important decision to someone else? You and your family have to get involved in finding the answers.

To make this tough question even more complicated, often there are two uncontrollable variables to the retirement question:

1. **Money** (How much you will earn and how much you will spend.)

2. **Lifespan** (How long you will live.)

The second variable, lifespan, is probably the one most outside of our control. We can tend to our diet and exercise and do the things that have been proven to help keep ourselves healthy, but in the end we have no guarantees. We have no control over how much time we will be granted or how long we have to buzz around on this planet.

The first variable, however, is one where there is an opportunity for more control, especially when it comes to how much you will spend. Unfortunately, after years of polishing their shopping and self-indulgence skills, it is difficult for some people, especially many Boomers, to restrict their spending. With the ease of credit, it is not unusual for them to actually spend more than they earn!

It's all about control. *Self* control.

Ideally, how much you spend and how much you save and/or invest should be a balance of current and future needs. Deciding to buy only what you need, not what you want (or think you want) can require some discipline until new habits are formed. It also requires forgetting about the Joneses. As I've said, the Joneses don't care. Never have. Never will. Not even one teensy bit.

The Real Cost vs. The Price Tag

Consider the real cost of an item before you purchase it. Let's say for example, you spot an absolutely gorgeous vase. The price tag on it is $250 and you are tempted.

Well, if you are in a 50 percent tax bracket, that means you must earn $500 in order to have the $250 for the vase, as the first $250 goes to taxes. If you are in a 30 percent tax bracket, you must earn $358 in order to have $250 of after tax dollars. Does the vase still look as beautiful when you look at the "real" price?

The bottom line is you can't invest it if you can't save it. I'll always remember the words of Marion Boyle, a dear lady with a lifetime of wisdom in the words she wrote to me as her financial advisor: "I can stretch the pennies, Ken. You can stretch the dollars."

Here's a good rule of thumb—

- Save 10 percent of your household income.

- Use 20 percent to pay down your debt.

- Live on 70 percent of your income.

That means if your annual family income is $100,000 (after taxes) save $10,000, direct $20,000 to pay down your current debt and live on $70,000. That means each month

155

you have $5,833.33 to feed, clothe, shelter and take care of yourselves and your family. If your annual family income is $50,000 (after taxes) use the same percentages. Save $5,000, and use $10,000 to pay down current debt. That leaves you with $2,916.66 each month for the basic necessities. If that is less than you currently spend each month (in either case), you and your spouse need to put your heads together to find a way to make it work. Be creative! There is always a way.

You can do it yourself or work with a financial advisor to determine how much money you require to retire at the age and in the lifestyle you and your spouse desire. Then have a set stage of targets over time. Just don't say "We need 2 million by 2015 to retire." Start with achievable yearly targets for IRAs or RRSPs, Investment Accounts, RESPs, and mortgage repayments. Write them down in your binder under your "Goals" section.

Do the math, but try not to base it strictly on financial terms. Always remember why you are monitoring your money. If you have worthwhile or fun alternatives to look forward to at retirement, keep them in mind to help yourself remain motivated to stick to your Plan for Life.

Take the time to create a Life Plan with your partner. We all know that time is a scarce commodity. But this is so important to do that you simply must *make the time*. If you want time, you must make it. Grab your binder and your spouse and get away for the weekend and get it done. It doesn't need to be tedious or complicated.

It is never too late to do this. "I wish I'd read The Wealthy Barber 20 years ago" is the big, pathetic excuse for inaction *now*. Any plan is better than no plan.

"There is a time in the life of every problem when it is big enough to see, yet small enough to solve."
— Mike Leavitt

Ongoing Process

Life is an ongoing process, and so is your Life Plan. Once you and your partner have created your Binder, figured out your magical nut and your goals, and devised a plan as to how you will get there — *don't tuck it away in a drawer or a closet.* You know that old saying about something out of sight it is at risk of being out of mind? Out of mind is the exact opposite of what you want when it comes to the content of your Binder. You want the dreams and details contained in your Binder to become part of the fabric of your family life.

I suggest you review the contents often. It will help any restructuring you decide to do in your spending or saving habits. When I first began with my Binder I looked at it, and reread the contents thoroughly once each week, sometimes more often.

Review your Family Binder together once a month with your partner in the beginning, and no less than four times a year once you get the hang of things. Compare how you are doing with the targets you set.

Realize that new habits can take time to form, and deviating from the Plan is no excuse to throw it out in its entirety. It's like dieting — if you go off your diet one day, you'll not fail to achieve your goal weight if you simply get back on it the next day. Besides, it isn't the diet that causes weight loss. Weight loss is achieved by choices and actions in line with your goal. You fail only by abandoning the choices and actions that you know will help you reach your goals.

Use these review sessions to reaffirm your passion for The Plan by talking about what waits for you "at the end of the rainbow" if you stick to your Life Plan. Keep collecting pictures that represent your dreams and goals and place them in your Binder.

Remember to visualize — it is a powerful tool. Close your eyes and visualize yourself, your mate and your surroundings *how they will be* when you have achieved the goal. See it, feel it, hear it, smell it and taste it with as much detail as you can. My wife and I love tennis, so one of my favorite personal visualizations is of my wife and I retired, watching a new star unseat the previous tennis champion at Wimbledon. When I visualize this, *I am there*. I can see the crowd, hear the cheers and taste the ice cold beer we sip while we watch. We share these visualizations and it has always inspired us to stick to our plan. We know that if we make the decisions and take the actions outlined in our Life Plan, we will get there.

Treat these times together focused on your Life Plan as special occasions with your partner. They *are* special. My wife and I find that getting away without the kids allows us to focus on each other and our plans much more effectively. We do this twice a year, and we look forward to it each time. No parents could love their children more dearly than we do, but we really appreciate Grandma's offering to look after them while we get away for our seasonal Family Life Plan reviews. It is much easier to do without the distractions and demands of three very active young children.

You Gotta Believe

Never stop imagining and believing in your dreams and goals. Believing in your dream gives you the power to stay committed. You and your partner must believe in the process. It will never happen if you don't. That's why it is so important that the two of you work on a plan that is yours, and yours alone. You must know in your hearts that the goals, and schedules to achieve them, are realistic.

If you've worked out the numbers and the whole thing hinges on winning the lottery, you do not have what I would call a realistic plan. At the time of writing this book, there is a television campaign by a major financial institution that says 16 percent of their projected market actually think they are going to win the lottery (or receive a similar windfall) and that will be their retirement funds.

I hope that advertisement is a joke, but something tells me that 16 percent number didn't come from thin air. I guess either way — true or not — it is a joke. If that commercial resembles your financial plan, there is nothing funny about it, and I suggest you and your partner get yourselves a dose of reality. Your chances of winning a major lottery, in reality, is a fraction of one percent, making your chances somewhere between slim and nil. Don't you think you and your family deserve a better shot at being happy?

It is up to you to make it happen. And like life itself, it is a process. It takes time.

If fact, it takes all the time you've got, because it doesn't end until you pass on from this earth to meet your Maker (or whoever you expect you'll be meeting).

"Life is a Journey, not a destination."
—Anonymous

$\mathcal{W}$e-thinking and acting.

As we discussed in the last chapter, I am a strong proponent of marriage. The committed, lasting, together-forever kind of marriage. I think it is part of the best financial or Life Plan that you could ever have.

"We" language replaces "I" language in the kind of marriage I believe in. I strongly hold that if your are in a marriage, you are we. There is no I and you or me. There is a we. Together *we* decide what *we* will do. The actions may be carried out independently, (one looks after the kids while the other brings home the bacon) but it is with a spirit of the good of the relationship and family. And everything is shared — successes and failures — without personal blame or credit.

This is only possible in an atmosphere of 'we.' It doesn't really matter who scores for the team; it matters only that the team scores. If the goalkeeper lets one in, it is because the team broke down somewhere in its defense. The goalie can not accept total blame for the loss any more than he can accept total credit for a win. The same principle applies in marriage.

"The ideal marriage is not one in which two people marry to be happy, but to make each other happy."
—Roy L. Smith, 1887-1963, Methodist Minister

Let me ask you something. When you and your partner wrote out your goals and ambitions, did either of you include your aspirations for your relationship? If you did, good for you! But if you did not, you are not alone. For whatever reason, goals for the relationship rarely make the list without prompting or unless the relationship is already in jeopardy. But a good relationship is not something to be taken for granted. It deserves attention, and like anything else that is alive or living, it requires feeding and nurturing.

It's not only good for finances, a good relationship with your spouse is very important to your well-being, according to John Gottman, author of *Seven Principles for Making Marriage Work* (Crown Books) and psychologist at the University of Washington in Seattle. He says that less than wedded bliss increases the chance of illness by 35 percent and knocks four years off your life!

So if you overlooked relationship goals in your Life Plan, get back to your Binder with the love of your life and add your thoughts on the subject. What are the great things about your relationship with your spouse that you don't want to lose or take for granted? Write them down. What do you wish to improve about your relationship? Write it down. How will you go about it? Write it all down and, as always, sign it with your mate and add it into your Binder.

Resolving Differences

It almost goes without saying that any two people will discover differences between them. The real test of a relationship is how you talk through and work out the inevitable differences. There are no cut and dried answers, nor one standard formula that works for everyone. The key is to resolve differences in a way that both parties can live with. Both must be able to live with the decision and the consequences of it.

Sometimes it can take a lot of talking to reach that point. Make the effort because it is worth it. Be honest with each other and, at the same time, always remember the objective is to do what is best for the partners and the family. The dictionary is the only place that success comes before work. Ask yourselves: What is best for *us*? That's what I mean by "We-thinking and acting."

"Love is the only game that two can play —
and both can win!."
—Author Unknown

To be sure, sometimes sacrifices will be necessary. If discussions become deadlocked, in that neither of you is able to move over to the other partner's persuasion, you might want to explore a "meet in the middle" approach.

At first blush, this may seem that neither of you are getting what you want. By meeting in the middle, technically neither of you gets *exactly* what you wanted. But if meeting in the middle restores peace to the dinner table discussions and ultimately matches your overall objectives — you are winning!

It's all about compromise. Let's say it's been a wicked winter and one of you wants to get away for a couple of weeks and bask under a tropical sun. The other partner looks at the calendar, notices it is RRSP or IRA season and is of the opinion that the best thing they could do with the extra money right now would be to put it into an RRSP or IRA account. Which do you do?

Whenever possible, be creative in your discussions. Try to find a way that both of you get what you want. For example, in the above case, a great solution might be to sock the money you have right now into the RRSP or IRA account, and wait until April or May (when you get your income tax refund) and *then* take that much needed vacation. If the vacation can be delayed for a couple of months, both partner's wishes can be met.

This is a very simple example and one that is fairly easy to resolve. I realize that many real life situations are more complicated and points of resolution can be elusive. But if you keep talking in a spirit of good will and faith, the answers will come. They will often be in the form of a compromise. It takes maturity to be able to keep your eye on the ball and do this without resenting the compromises, but no more maturity than it takes to build a good marriage and stick to your Life Plan.

The rewards are multiple. Not only will you and your mate achieve your ultimate goals, you will be teaching your children (who are always watching) some priceless life skills. They will learn that it is okay to have differences of opinion. More importantly, they will learn that conflicts can be resolved with meaningful dialogue. Good on you!

Tips from the Field

I am not a marriage counselor, and I do not profess to have all the answers. But my wife Shawna and I have a great relationship that we have worked hard at building. Along the way we've discovered some principles and habits that really work for us. I offer them to you, and I hope they work as well for you as they do for us.

1. *Believe in each other and your marriage.*

Believe you will be together for life. And make sure your partner knows how much you care, and that you are in it for the long haul.

2. *Trust one another.*

Trust takes time to establish and has to be earned. Continually work at it to keep it.

3. *Keep your daily/weekly/yearly habits aligned with your Family Philosophy.*

4. *It's okay not to be perfect.*

Not everything goes as planned. I had a hard, hard time realizing this. Shawna, my wife, had to work with me and coach me. Accepting less than perfection was a major breakthrough. The more kids we had, the easier it became. Dropping the perfection attitude was a major habit that had to be discussed and changed. It took a long time to realize that not being perfect was okay.

5. Be each other's biggest fan.

Support each other. Cheer each other on. Tell each other compliments frequently and regularly. Appreciate each other.

Note: If one of the partners is more of a believer than the other, the stronger believer must take the lead for the family. Run the ball with enthusiasm! Over time, as results are achieved and appreciated, one by one the whole family will be with you. All it takes is time. You have all there is!

> *"The quality of our life is in direct relation to the quality of our relationships."*
> Anthony Robbins

Enjoy the Journey.

If, as one of my favorite quotes suggests — life is a journey not a destination— then it follows that in order to enjoy life, what we must do is simple — *enjoy the journey*. To enjoy life means to enjoy the journey. The choice, like all others, is ours to make.

It all hinges on attitude, remember? And quite literally, we can choose our polarity. We can choose to have a happy disposition or a mean one. We can choose to enjoy life or we can endure it. We can choose to be optimistic or we can choose to be pessimistic. If you are not sure which camp you wish to be in, let me tell you some pretty interesting and recent research results on the subject before you make your decision.

Dozens of recent studies show that optimists do better than pessimists at pretty much everything that could be measured. Optimism (the curious human habit of expecting good things to happen, often in defiance of reality) helps us do better at work, school and sports. Optimists suffer less depression, achieve more goals, and respond better to stress.

And there's more.

When optimists did become ill, they were more effective at battling the disease. Not only did they get better faster, they produced more incidents of completely recuperating from a serious affliction. Overall, optimistic people also live longer. As I said, there is plenty of supporting evidence for optimism, the enjoyment of life and the belief in yourselves and your dreams.

There is one exception.

Where risk is involved, excessive optimism can be dangerous. Epidemics of sexually transmitted diseases, for example, are fueled in part by people who make overly optimistic assumptions about their sexual partners. There are many other instances in which people's under-estimation of risk can get them into serious trouble. Day trading, speculative investments, costly get-rich-quick schemes and wildly optimistic ROIs (Return on Investments) are a few examples that come to mind.

But wherever serious risk is not a factor, it is clearly to our benefit to maintain a positive, optimistic outlook.

We will have more fun and we will be more fun to be around. Life for us and those around us will be more enjoyable.

Having Fun is Important

Enjoyment and fun can be overlooked as easily as a good relationship can be taken for granted. With the demands of careers, children, families and life in general, having fun can be shuffled low on the priority list when, according to some experts, it should be very close to the top of the list. I have been told of a very effective treatment center in Wickenburg, Arizona for alcohol and drug addiction that believes a neglected "Right to Have Fun" is one of the things that creates a life imbalance. That, in turn, contributes to life problems. We all have a need to have fun, according to the professionals at the center, and if we neglect to address this need it will cause problems for us in our lives.

Don't live just to accomplish goals, as is the plight of unhappy workaholics. Certainly you must take responsibility for reaching your objectives and that can take a lot of focus and determination. But always remember the value of balance in your life. Work hard when you work, but regularly plan times for yourself and for your family activities that are just plain and simple fun. They need not be expensive. In fact, they don't need to cost anything at all. Family walks in the park, bike rides, board games, gathering together to watch a spectacular sunset (or sunrise), are all fun and free. All work and no play makes Jack and Jane . . . miserable. Make time for fun with your spouse and with your family.

> *"Happiness is not a state to arrive at,*
> *but rather a manner of traveling."*
> —Anonymous

Reward yourself (wisely).

Track results against goals, and once you have hit targets, *reward yourselves*. Relish and cherish these times. They symbolize your success, and all that it took for the two of you to achieve it. It took focus, determination and even sacrifice at times, but you did it! Enjoy and savor the feelings with each other. It is important to recognize your progress and reward it.

Celebrate your successes with a reward that is meaningful and appropriate. Do it wisely, with your eye on your ultimate goals and plans for yourselves. In other words, don't get so carried away that you blow the budget. The key word here is appropriate.

Big Hat, No Cattle

An expensive automobile was, at one time, a grand signal of success. Without saying a word, it announced to the neighborhood: "*I have done well and I am successful. My family is well taken care of. My financial house is in order so I am indulging myself with this new car.*" In all likelihood, the car was paid for outright. The thinking was, that if you couldn't pay cash for the car, you could not afford it. If you couldn't afford it, you waited and saved until you did.

Boy, has that changed!

To the delight (and profit) of automobile makers, a car now seems to be rather high on the priority or reward list, if not right at the top. The concept of paying cash for a luxury car has all but disappeared to the average North American. In fact, the very concept of automobile ownership itself is almost lost, having been replaced with 'convenient' leasing arrangements.

The auto industry had to do this. When it noticed that sales were steadily dropping (probably because of the high cost of such cars) they engaged some creativity in their boardrooms and came out with a new way to move cars off their lots — lease them. The market, largely made up of Boomers always anxious for 'instant gratification,' responded warmly to the leasing concept and that is how most cars are moved off the lot today. In reality, a luxury car now signals nothing more than the driver has qualified for the monthly lease payments. I have a favorite phrase for this (foolish) tendency to display the trappings without the substance — *Big hat, no cattle!*

Please don't get me wrong. I am not anti-luxury cars. I like to drive a nice car just as much as the next fellow. What I can not support is the incurring of additional debt (which is what a lease is) without a solid financial foundation. I happen to believe that the thousands of dollars spent each year on a luxury car lease would often be better placed in financial instruments — IRAs or RRSPs, or investment accounts — where it will grow and support the key goals and dreams of a Life Plan. No one has yet been able to explain to me how a leased luxury car gets you closer to your goals if it is done at the expense of responsible financial planning.

Live Like a Millionaire

My advice? I say buy the big hat *after* you've acquired the cattle. Call me old fashioned if you like, but there are others who agree with me. They may be old fashioned too, but they are also millionaires.

When they hear the word millionaire, many people conjure up pictures of jetting away to Paris for lunch, dining on caviar, shopping in the most expensive boutiques and endless games of golf or tennis. But in reality, most millionaires live a different, relatively modest lifestyle.

According to the bestseller *The Millionaire Next Door*, millionaires are twice as likely to shop at Sears as Saks Fifth Avenue and would rather eat sandwiches than caviar.

Millionaires are not consumption crazy. They have their shoes resoled or repaired and have their furniture reupholstered or refinished instead of buying new. They almost always prepare a list before they go shopping (nearly half shop with coupons they've clipped) and almost half leave the store immediately after completing the intended purchase. Their priorities are: time with their family and friends, paying off mortgages and any debt early, and financial planning, especially expert tax planning. They spend a great deal of time researching opportunities with their financial professional.

Not at all like the common perception of millionaires!

Experts say the real reason people get rich is that they live below their means. This is so obvious, yet so uncommon. They (millionaires) constantly ask themselves

"What will give me the most pleasure for the least expense?"

That is particularly true when it comes to buying a car. Forty percent of millionaires surveyed for the book said they drove a used one, claiming that buying a new car is like throwing money away. They'd rather buy a quality used car and invest the savings. That's how they get richer.

You can save $5,000 or more if you buy a two-year old car instead of the same one brand-new. Well invested at say, 12 percent, the money you save on the purchase price could double (in the stock market) in 6 years. The value of a six-year old car is never double its original price!

Most of the lifestyle activities of the wealthy are very different from the lavish lifestyles that people imagine about them. Lavish, or pseudo-affluent lifestyles are actually more common among non-millionaires with high incomes than among first-generation millionaires.

That could explain why most high-living people rarely become wealthy. These are the people with real big hats and no cattle. Giving the impression of wealth is more important to them than actually accumulating wealth. Poor souls! Someone forgot to tell them that the Joneses (or anybody else for that matter) really don't care.

If future wealth is one of your goals, then the best advice I could give you is: live like a millionaire! Enjoy your family and friends, live below your means and stick to your Life Plan.

Use the formula for **POWER:**

Plan for Life is an

On going Process of

We-thinking and acting.

Enjoy the journey, and

Reward yourself wisely.

Pass on the P-O-W-E-R to your children. You'll be teaching your future grandchildren!

"Some succeed because they are destined to, most succeed because they are determined to."

—Anonymous

Chapter 7 Review

- We have the power to do and be whatever is within our capability.

- Without a plan, we are planning to fail.

- Life is an ongoing process. It is a journey, not a destination.

- We-thinking and acting help keep a marriage together.

- Having fun is important.

- It's good to reward ourselves when we reach our goals.

Chapter Eight

﷯

There is a Difference Between
Gambling and Investing

Chapter Eight

There is a Difference Between Gambling and Investing

"It is an old and ironic habit of human beings to run faster when we have lost our way."
—Anonymous

There are really only four ways we can make money. Five, if you include counterfeiting, which for obvious reasons I don't. Other than that (counterfeiting is something I could never condone) we have only four available options when it comes to how we make money.

1. We can earn it.

Most of us make money by working for it. We've become a society of working people. Men, women, young, old — we all work. Youngsters get part time jobs delivering newspapers; high school youth work after school and on weekends. Men work. Women work. We hold jobs, engage in careers, or become self-employed and run our own business. And seniors, once seen only on golf courses and knitting clubs are reporting for duty in the service sector in growing numbers.

We work, work, work. To make money, money, money. Trouble is, most of the money we make, make, make goes to pay bills, bills, bills.

2. We could receive a windfall.

Another way we can make money is to receive an inheritance or other windfall.

Everyone wants to be a millionaire. Or marry one, as evidenced by the FOX Network *"Who Wants to Marry a Millionaire"* debacle in February 2000. There was no shortage of contestants, or viewers. Networks across the country scrambled to produce and broadcast *their* version of Everyone Wants to Be a Millionaire. Audiences couldn't get enough of it, it seemed. Everyone wants to become a millionaire. And we want to become one instantly.

There are now more millionaires in the United States than ever before, on a per capita basis. (The Game Shows aren't the reason!) And the numbers grow daily. It is estimated there are 60 new millionaires per day. At last count, there were almost 10 million (9.8) millionaires in the United States. It is interesting to note that there are also about the same number (10 million) adults on the other end of the spectrum, who have so little money they don't even have a bank account.

Who hasn't dreamed of being rich? We buy lottery tickets and fantasize what we'll do with the millions, should we win them. Every once in a while we'll hear or read a story about some serendipitous guy who finds a huge whack of cash while walking his dog and we wonder if that will ever happen to us. Or if one day we'll find out an old heirloom is really a Van Gogh. Or if we'll inherit it out of the blue from a rich unknown relative.

It *might* happen, right? Yeah, it might. And someday, money might grow on trees, too. And pigs might fly.

3. We can steal it.

Well, we could. But then, there's that reality of getting caught, going to jail and that pretty much wipes out stealing as a viable way to make money. Enough said.

4. We can invest in something.

Yes. Yes. Yes.

Investing is a way to make money grow. Providing we can save it (and we *can*, if we so choose), we can use that money to make more money. Investing is a way for money that we've earned working at our jobs and businesses, continue to work for us by increasing in value, earning interest, or dividends, and allowing us to benefit from the compounding effect. Wisely invested, our money can earn more money for us.

The question is how to invest wisely.

The Wise Investor

Everyone wants to do the right thing when it comes to investing money. No one in their right mind makes an investment and says, "Gee, I hope I lose money on this one." Quite the contrary. When we make an investment, it is with the expectation that the value of the money we have invested will increase.

This would all be so much easier if we each had a crystal ball. We could all then gaze into it and be able to spot the winners (which we'd eagerly invest in) and the losers (which we would obviously avoid like the plague). But the reality is that we don't have a crystal ball. No one knows the future with an absolute certainty. Anyone who tells you they do is seriously misinformed.

But that doesn't mean for you to throw caution to the wind or the wolves, and get out your dart board to pick your investments. There are basic considerations for any investment, regardless of market conditions or anything else.

Here are some questions to ask yourself :

1. Does it fit with my overall plan?

2. Over what period of time will my money be in this investment? And does it fit with my overall plan?

3. Is the level of risk safe enough for me, practically and emotionally? And, does it fit with my overall plan?

Investment Rule #1

Have A Plan.

First of all, you need a plan. Investing is not about hit and miss chance-taking. That's gambling. Investing is different than gambling. Investing requires a series of actions and activities taken toward a goal over an established period of time. That necessitates a plan. If that isn't already obvious to you, please reread the chapters leading up to this one, because you've missed a major point. Not having a plan is like planning to fail.

Like anything else important, your investing activity will benefit from a thoughtful blueprint. Having a plan makes subsequent decisions possible and easier. Are you making this investment to sock money away for the future, or does your situation require that it generate income for you to take care of your month-to-month needs? Of course, age is usually a factor here, but there are other considerations specific to *your* individual situation.

Unless you can afford the time to become an expert yourself, involve a financial professional to help you establish the guidelines that are best for you. The length of time money will be held in an investment (sometimes called the horizon line), must be considered. Is yours five years? 10? 15? 30? Again, your age is a factor, but there are other elements to consider, such as what else is in your investment portfolio. The input and counsel of a dedicated, objective financial professional should be sought. Listen to their input and make your decisions according to *your own* overall, long term financial plan.

We say we can handle risk, but...

Risk, and our ability to deal with it, is a big consideration when making investment decisions. We may be tempted to quickly glaze over the risk factor, thinking "Oh well, risk is part of any investment." While it is true that risk is inherent, not paying due consideration to our own personal risk tolerance is like a disaster waiting to happen.

There are two levels to weigh when evaluating the potential risk. First of all, we must assess whether we can handle it from a practical side. What assets could be affected? Seriously play the "What If" game. What are the consequences if things don't go as planned? Can you handle it?

And secondly, we must evaluate our ability to manage the emotions implicit with risk. Because you can be sure there will be moments and phases during market turns that can make riding the highest roller coaster feel like the Teacup Ride at Disneyland. You need to seriously and honestly assess and accept your personal risk comfort zone when devising your investment plan. Your assessment of your ability to handle risk must be unpretentious, or there will be too many agonizing days ahead for you, your mate, your family and your poor financial advisor. More than one relationship could easily become tarnished.

My experience is that when people meet with their financial professional, a big majority say they can tolerate significant risk. Perhaps this is what they think is the correct answer. Or the one the person on the other side of the table wants to hear. Whatever the reason, almost all claim to have nerves of steel and to have a nearly sky-high risk tolerance.

Hmmm....

The curious thing is that when queried by someone outside the financial services industry, almost half (46 percent) of the people asked confide being *reluctant to take any investment risk at all!* Only about one-fifth (20 percent) are willing to take above-average risks to earn above-average investment returns, and this percentage drops drastically the older the respondent. Only seven percent of persons aged 65 and over say they are willing to take such risk.

Opportunity almost always involves some risk. It is something you won't be able to avoid completely. My advice to you is determine how much risk is *too much for you*. Get an accurate handle on your level of tolerance for risk, and the effects it has on you and your personality. Honestly determine your tolerance and accept it. If you can't handle it, you can't handle it. There is nothing wrong or deficient about a low risk tolerance. Some people have an amazing tolerance for pain. Others don't. It's okay, whichever way you lean. What is NOT okay is pretending you can handle more risk than reality.

Risk makes some people lean so far they tilt.

Another reason I urge you to candidly assess your risk tolerance is because risk makes some people lean so far they tilt. Folks with a low risk tolerance will suffer so much anxiety during market corrections (which are as certain to occur as the Law of Gravity) that they become, well let's call it over stressed. They become miserable with worry, doubt and fear. That can't help but effect the family balance, and it is never in a good way.

And ditto for the relationship with their financial advisor. If you have their office on speed dial every time the market hiccups, you have overstated your risk tolerance. You are very quickly going to become one of his/her least favorite people to talk to, and who can blame them? Their job is not to hold your hand 24 hours a day.

Another example of personalities who tilt with risk are a little more difficult to spot. Because at first, they seem to be really able to handle it. In fact, they seem to enjoy it. They find it stimulating, thrilling or somehow energizing.

Only they like it too much. These folks are drawn to day trading like a magnet, and what starts out as a harmless hobby can become a dangerous compulsion. Driven by obsessive behavior, these folks confuse investing with gambling.

Always remember that gambling and investing are two different things. If you become overly excited by risk, be careful. Allocate as much money to your highly speculative adventures as you would to gambling, or entertainment. Because that's what it is. I'm not saying don't do it. I'm just saying call a spade a spade.

It's tricky when partners in a marriage have different levels of risk tolerance, as often is the case. One partner might be well suited to it, the other becomes a quivering mess at the mere rumor of a market downturn. Just in case you are wondering, gender has no bias when it comes to risk. I've met about as many women as men who truly have high levels of risk tolerance. Equally, I've met as many men as women who couldn't handle it at all.

If there are differences, partners must work it out to create a financial plan that they can *both* live with comfortably. Once again, it is helpful to involve a financial professional to help you work out a balance that suits both partners level of comfort. The key is to develop a plan. That's the first rule of investing — have a plan.

Investment Rule #2

Don't Put All Your Eggs In One Basket.

If you have 10 baskets, and you put all of your eggs in one of them, you'd lose all your eggs if that basket met with unforeseen misfortune (as if there is any other kind of misfortune). But if you put one egg in each basket, you'd only lose one egg if that basket was wiped out. It is a simple concept— don't put all your eggs in one basket.

The phrase itself is well known and pretty commonly accepted in the financial industry and in business. I was curious where it came from and half expected it to have roots in some nice children's story. So you can imagine my surprise when I saw the title *Don Quixote* by Miguel de Cervantes (1547-1616) associated with the origins of the phrase.

"It is the part of a wise man
to keep himself today for tomorrow,
and not venture all his eggs in one basket."
—Don Quixote (Part 1, Book 111, Chapter 9)
by Miguel de Cervantes,
Bartlett's Familiar Quotations

Definitely not children's bedtime material! But what delighted me most, and caused me to grin was the mention of tomorrow and today. It mirrors our concept that tomorrow never lies. Those words hold as much truth today as they did in the 16th century. But then, wisdom often has a long shelf life.

Never put *most* of your eggs into one basket either. Not unless you can afford the loss, both financially and emotionally. Some people risk far too much on one particular stock or investment. They put too many eggs in one basket and experience disaster when the stock or mutual fund tanks.

How much is too much?

That depends. The factors that must be considered are your risk tolerance and your horizon line, or the number of years in your investment period. If you are young with a long horizon line, I don't think 25 percent is unrealistic. It is pushing the upper end of what I would recommend, but if you can handle the risk, go for it. However, if you can't handle the risk or have a shorter time line, 25 percent is probably too much. Ten to 15 percent is a more realistic figure. And if you have only a handful of years until retirement, the percentage should be even less.

"Only a fool tests the depth of the water with both feet."

—Anonymous

Rules For Investing #3

Don't Fiddle With Your Funds.

Do not confuse motion and progress. A rocking horse keeps moving but does not make any progress. Studies have shown that people who constantly fiddle with their funds do not do as well as those who have a plan and stick to it. There's those magic words again— have a plan and stick to it.

People, I want to tell you something— you are shooting yourselves in the foot by flit flit flitting from fund to fund. Studies show that people who are constantly flit in and out of funds don't do as well as the funds themselves. Just how badly they lag behind was the subject of a study by DALBAR, Inc., a Boston-based consulting firm. According to the analysis of buying patterns, which covered the period from March, 1990 to December, 1999, investors on average are not making anywhere near the returns of the funds. This is largely due to bouncing in and out of funds.

The comparative return for the Morgan Stanley World index, which was used as a proxy for the typical foreign equity fund, rose a total of 313 percent in the study period. On a compound annual basis, according to DALBAR, Inc., the average investor's return was only 7.34 percent, compared with 15.52 percent annually for the world index. Domestic Equities presented a similar picture. It is interesting to note that, despite the negative result of fund jumping, the average holding time for mutual funds is getting shorter in both Canada and the United States.

Studies have shown that people who invest regularly in the same investments do significantly better in the long run than those who bounce in and out. So unless a fund under performs similar funds for three years, stay put.

From time to time you should examine your basket of investments (asset allocation) and compare it with your original target. Rebalancing may be in order. Rarely is wholesale change required. Yet few people rebalance their portfolios, and far too many engage in wholesale change on a frequent or routine basis. Go figure! The Investment Advisor makes money, but the client does not by using this strategy.

Rules For Investing #4

At The End Of The Day, The Market Will Reward Companies That Make Money.

If you've been listening lately, there's been much talk about whether or not this is a new economy. People are asking each other "What's going to happen? Will the internet change *everything*?"

It is not the first time that question — Is this a new economy? — has been raised. And it probably is not the last. Predictions are rampant. They always are, in this business.

We began the new millennium with quite a range of forecasts. We had the savant Mark Holowesko, who took over the reins of the Templeton Growth Fund from Sir John Templeton, quoted as calling the period www.bubble.com and predicted 90 percent of all internet stocks would fall 90 percent. Sir John Templeton himself was quoted at the same time as saying it was the greatest bubble he'd ever witnessed.

We had e-commerce people telling us that we could no longer use historical measurements such as price to book, price to earnings ratios and that we should use a new valuation based on future cash flow and new accounting principles. We had IPO's go from $25.00 on the first day of trading to $200 and beyond. No one had ever seen this before and it created a frenzy of investors bulging at the seams with their appetite for high tech stocks. Wealthy investors were not exempt from the tidal wave and many succumbed to an infatuation with hedge funds. Everyone became an overnight expert, an attitude easily assumed in a buoyant bull market.

One of my favorite cartoons that surfaced at the time showed a client meeting with his Investment Professional. The client is happily telling his advisor — *"I'm not unrealistic like all those dot comers. I'll be happy with 70 or 80 percent return!"*

As it turned out, many were left feeling that most hedge funds were little more than an opportunity for overpaid money managers to gamble with other people's money. And many IPO's were likened to pyramid schemes, in that the only people who really made any serious money were those at the inner or presidents circle. By the time the offering reached the average guy, profits were not as swift, nor as handsome. Not even close. If there were any profits at all!

"If you see a bandwagon, it's too late."
—Sir James Goldsmith

It took investors a little time to realize that their optimism exceeded inevitable reality. Human nature seems to be like that. Sometimes it takes us a while to accept something we would rather not be true. Until then, it was gold rush days and the fever spread fast like a bad smell. Fueled by media reports of fortunes being made overnight, we became crazed for wildly high expectations.

None were higher than Wanda P.'s expectations. On December 31, 1999 her account value was $154,957. Two months later she was up 56 percent ($87,000) for a total of $242,000. She'd gone into a high tech stock and won! Instead of seeing it for what it was (a lucky break), her thinking became clouded. In her elation, you'd have thought that Wanda was having a spiritual experience. Wanda became overexcited. Her new plan? Trade more frequently!

"My account should be worth $400,000 in 9 months!" she exclaimed in delight.

How did she arrive at this amazing revelation? With what could kindly be called fuzzy logic.

Drawing on her experience as the owner of a small decorating business, Wanda crunched some numbers. She'd made $87,000 in a two month period. *At that rate*, in a 9 month period, her account would grow to roughly $400,000. At a consistent growth rate of 56 percent, her numbers were correct. The problem was, the odds were about as good as the odds of Wanda winning the lottery four or five times in a row! Her Financial Advisor attempted to point this out to her, but she would have none of it.

"I don't know what I'm doing, I know that. But I'm running with this anyway!" she declared, smug with the belief that she could circulate with the movers and shakers who would provide more "hot tips."

I spoke with her husband a few months later, and the news was not good. Apparently subsequent "hot tips" did not work out quite so well.

"It has been a very humbling experience...for both of us," he said. Maybe it was a spiritual experience after all.

Craze was an accurate word to describe the Dot Com Fever that afflicted many investors. But it wasn't the first time people have been there, either. How many people would put their money in "*a company for carrying on an undertaking of great advantage, but no one to know what it is?*" You might laugh, but in the 18th century 1,000 shares were sold in just such a London venture. It raised 2,000 pounds for its founder, a very significant amount in the 1700s. By the way, he then promptly took off for the Continent, and was never heard of again.

And then there was the South Sea Bubble that ruined thousands in the 1720s who were lured by visions of wealth in South America's gold and silver mines. We've had a history of such enticements, including the early railways, cars and a host of other projects of their time.

Underlying all market mania is the Greater Fool Principle: *Even if you know a scheme is ill-founded, enough idiots will buy into it for you to win.*

This was obviously known to the inventors of www.iTulip.com. The web site was founded in 1998 as a parody of an e-commerce firm and highlighted the trend's resemblance to the tulip craze in Europe in the 1600s that was created purely on sentiment not substance (sound familiar?). "Buy an iTulip.com stock certificate," it prompted visitors to the site. "Not only does iTulip.com not have any assets, revenues or profits, it doesn't even exist." Stock certificates went on sale from $10.95 and... you guessed it! As I said, the frenzy was everywhere.

Eventually there was a problem, as there always is with bubble economies. Most of the hot dot-coms were only making money out of the same mechanisms that apply in pyramid schemes. What I means is the money being 'made' was actually the money of the investors that followed. It wasn't money made by the dot-com business. Duh! Maybe that is why so many never, ever showed a profit.

This should always be an investment warning signal. All pyramid systems eventually collapse when the number of lemmings entering is not enough to sustain the illusion. Compounding the treachery of these times was artificial dollars being used to buy hard assets, as we witnessed when AOL purchased Time Warner.

When people started asking where the market was heading next, I maintained my traditional belief that forms my fourth rule for investing. That rule is simple: *At the end of the day the market will reward companies that make money.* Methods may change, technology will advance, and new ways of doing things will evolve. But in the end, I believe substance will prevail.

In the Real World, Mistakes Happen.

*"The problem is not
that there are problems.
The problem is expecting otherwise
and thinking that having a problem is a problem."*
—Anonymous

I've never met a person who liked screwing up. Nobody likes making mistakes. About the only person I can think of who can count on hearing a resounding cheer when he makes a mistake, is a goalie playing an away game. When he "lets one get by him," his mistake makes a lot of people happy. Maybe even thrilled.

But the applause is not music to his ears, because the cheers are coming from the wrong people! When a goalie makes a mistake, it's the *other* guys who cheer. Not his mates. Not his fans. Not the people who matter to him. Those are the cheers we want to hear most — the cheers from people we love and who matter to us. When it comes right down to it, they are the *only* ones we *care* about hearing.

Is it any wonder then, that when we make a mistake it can be so painful? It hurts. It hurts our pride, our pocketbook or both, depending on the severity of the mistake. Mistakes are like that. They can be downright painful. Frustrating. Costly. Crushing. In serious situations, they can be debilitating. Those are all normal reactions.

193

Well, try this on for size: Mistakes can also be invigorating. Energizing. Stimulating.

"Trouble is only opportunity in work clothes."
— Henry J. Kaiser

Mistakes can be opportunities. In fact, opportunities frequently come disguised as problems. Problems get people thinking about solutions. Real solutions cause an overall improvement. Once the dust settles, things are better than they were before the 'problem' that caused the 'solution' and change. Without the 'problem,' a solution would not have been sought (because we didn't know there was a problem). So, in a way, the problem was a good thing. If that sounds optimistic, well, that's my point — it's not what you call it, it's how you react to it that matters.

"A bend in the road is not the end of the road unless you fail to make the turn."
—Anonymous

I'm not crazy about calling anything a problem. Personally, I like using the word challenge. I say it is only a problem if you think it is a problem. But I have no quarrel with folks who prefer to call a spade a spade and a problem a problem. Because it doesn't matter what name you give it. Whatever you call it — problem, mistake, obstacle or opportunity — what matters is how you react to it. Sound familiar?

What makes the difference is our attitude.

Our attitude is where the power comes from to deal with difficult situations. We can choose to adopt a defeatist attitude, throw up our hands or throw in the towel and say "I give up. Oh well, I tried, but it didn't work. Poor me."

Or, we can dig down deep and find the character traits that we need. The ones that won't let us quit, that give us bounce and recovery. They are there.

A hand lettered sign at a playoff hockey game, in which the home team was the underdog, made this point another way. The sign was proudly held up by a beaming fan after his team had made yet another remarkable comeback. The sign read:

"Adversity does not build character. It reveals it."

We have all been told when things haven't gone our way that adversity builds character. Maybe it does. After we've come through a difficult time, we can realize just how strong and resourceful we are. We can gain confidence and wisdom, and many other qualities. Adversity can bring out many things. But for sure — the first thing adversity does is reveal and demonstrate character.

Make Sure it's Really a Problem.

"Rule No. 1 is, don't sweat the small stuff.
Rule No. 2 is, it's all small stuff."
—Robert Eliot

The first thing you want to do is make sure that what you think is a problem . . . *is really a problem*. That may sound too simplistic, but it isn't. Not in my experience. As humans, we are quite capable of construing something as a problem, when it really isn't.

Just because it isn't perfect doesn't mean it is a mistake.

Make sure that you really have a problem before you react as if you do. I want to quickly touch on this, because it is something I had to work on with myself. I'm a perfectionist (or recovering perfectionist). I nearly drove myself nuts when things didn't work out perfectly.

I reacted as if less than perfect meant it was a mistake. Fortunately for me, my wife Shawna helped me see the difference between reality (where things are rarely perfect) and an actual mistake. This was difficult for me to learn. Although, the more kids we had, the easier it became.

How to Deal with Problems and Setbacks

Life will have its share of problems and you will make mistakes. It's inevitable. They may be investment related or they may occur in other areas of your life. If they do, here are my suggestions for how to deal with it.

1. Accept it.

It happened. It can't be changed. Accept it. The sooner you can get to this point of acceptance, the better. I know that part of being human is experiencing feelings and emotions, and setbacks can bring them to a level of intensity never before felt. But the reality is the faster we can work through them and get past the situation, the better it is for us.

Sometimes it is a process. If the loss is severe, you may find the stages similar to that of grieving — denial (this is not happening), then anger (how could this happen to me, and who is to blame for it), followed by the next stage of self pity (why me), and finally that of acceptance.

"In three words I can sum up everything I've learned about life. It goes on."

— Robert Frost

2. Keep your eye on the ball.

Keep focused on the dream, the goal, the original objective. A good reminder of these can always be found in your Life Plan Binder. Keep these thoughts foremost in your mind. Push away any thoughts of regret, or anything related to it. Do not dwell on all the could haves, should haves, and would haves. You've lost the battle, maybe, but you are still in the game. It's only when you quit that you have really lost. If you don't quit, you still have a chance. Get back in it and play to win.

Remember your original objective, and why you wanted it in the first place. Provided the reasons have not changed, the goal is still attainable. You may need to find another way, but chances are the goal is still get-able.

"Success is how high you bounce when you hit bottom."
—Gen. George Patton

3. Learn from mistakes, and keep your pointing finger in your pocket.

Often when things go wrong, a strong reaction is to find someone to blame. We want to point a finger at the ogre, the jerk or the fool that got us into this mess. (If at first you don't succeed, set the blame fast.) We rarely think of the guy in the mirror as being at fault.

Apparently men are more apt to lay blame when things go afoul than are women. In a mixed gender study of managers, participants were asked to perform tasks with a team. They were told there would be an evaluation period afterward, but the managers were not told the real objective of the study — which was to see how they handled poor versus good reviews.

When told their group performed well, the typical male manager's response was, "Yeah, thanks, it was a good job." Men found it easy to accept credit for positive outcomes. Women, on the other hand were more likely to deflect the good review to their team members. Their typical response was, "I had great people to work with."

Both men and women reacted differently when told their group had performed poorly. The women were quick to criticize themselves. Men, in contrast, were quick to point at outside sources, a place or a person to lay blame for the failure. "I was given substandard team mates. We'd have done better if we had more time. It wasn't my fault," were common male responses.

You can't do that in a relationship. When a family experiences setbacks, forget about whose fault it is. That won't change a thing anyway. Figure out what went wrong, learn from it, and move past it.

4. Reach for each other.

If you have a partner, you are lucky. Most things are easier with two, and suffering setbacks is definitely easier with a partner. IF you remember that you are both in this together. If, on the other hand, you direct your anger (one of the stages to acceptance) at each other, neither of you will benefit.

Try hard, very hard not to do this. Find another outlet for any anger that you may be experiencing. When I'm upset I go for a run. I have found this helpful for "blowing off" excess emotion. Some researchers have said that upper body motion is best for blowing off anger. So pound a pillow. Get a punching bag. Take up boxing. Whatever works for you!

In times of trouble, you need each other. Be there for each other. If you momentarily lose your self-discipline, tell the other person. "I'm sorry, that came out all wrong..." will go a long way to diffusing friction. It is possible for relationships to grow stronger by weathering storms together. This won't happen if you *turn on* each other (I'm not talking attraction here) rather than *turning toward* each other.

5.   Be gentle with yourself.

You must be willing to allow yourself to make mistakes. Show me someone who has never made a mistake, and most likely you will be showing me someone who hasn't done anything. If you are in action, if you are *doing*, you will make a mistake eventually. It comes with the territory of being human. No one is perfect. No one.

Just remember that *you* are not a mistake. Maybe you made an error in judgment, but that doesn't make *you* a mistake. Most of all, try not to dwell on it. Some people find it hard to forgive themselves, and will engage in self-destructive self-talk. ("Boy, am I ever an idiot. How could I have been so stupid. I should have seen it coming. I knew better. What was I thinking...",etc., etc.) Push these thoughts and conversations with yourself out of your mind. They serve no useful purpose. Let go of the mistake and focus on your plan of action.

6. Control the damage.

In serious situations, damage control may be necessary. You may need to address related situations with action. Do so directly, and don't even consider avoidance behavior. You may run, but you'll never be able to hide.

You won't be able to effectively act if you get caught in the stages of anger, denial or self pity. So even if you feel like wallowing in self pity, it may not be a luxury you can afford. Sometimes you have to put your feelings on hold, or in your pocket while you deal with the damage control. You can always get back to the self pity or anger later. Yes, this will take a tremendous amount of self-discipline. Be up for the challenge!

7. Focus on what is going right, what makes things work.

Sometimes we can get too caught up in analyzing our mistakes. Disproportionate amounts of time are spent figuring out what happened, and why, and how it could have been avoided in the first place. While it is good to learn from mistakes, it is not good to overanalyze the situation. Direct your focus to what IS working in your lives.

In times of setbacks, it is even more important to lift your spirit to a positive frame of mind. It may not be easy to do, at first, but it will be the most beneficial if you can. Especially if your partner has taken the setback harder than you. Help each other to look at the positive. The stronger of the two of you might have to take the lead.

8. If the situation warrants, obtain professional help.

If the situation warrants it, waste no time in seeking the services of a professional. Embarrassed? Don't be. We all hit rough spots where we need help to cope with a situation. That's what these professionals do; that's why they are there. Use them. They can help.

I was 29 when my parents split up, and I was stunned by their break up. I knew things weren't perfect, but what marriage is without occasional discord? I thought my parents would be together forever. It was a big shock to me that it was not to be.

What made it even worse, was when both Mom and Dad began trying to polarize the kids, including me. Pretty soon I wasn't sure who was talking to whom, and it hit me that it was all having a negative effect on me.

"These people are confusing the living heck out of me!" I realized one day. I decided to talk to someone, and remembered a retired Catholic priest I knew. I thought he could help me and he did. He helped me put it all in perspective.

If you think it will help, never be reluctant to seek professional help of any kind, including legal, if that is what is required. Do not let embarrassment prevent you from doing this. I say this again, because it is common to think "I should have known better," or "That was such a stupid thing I did, I don't dare tell anyone." You know what? Con artists *count* on their victims being too embarrassed to say anything. Surprise them by seeking remedy, if the situation merits.

Even The Experts Make Mistakes

Everyone makes mistakes. Even the experts can be wrong. Once a year Berkshire Hathaway Chairman Warren Buffet releases a letter to shareholders. In 1998, on the first trading day after it was published McDonald's stock (MCD NYSE) dropped 3 percent. This was directly attributed to Buffet's disclosure the previous day that Berkshire had sold at least part of its stake in the world's largest restaurant chain.

However, it turned out that McDonald stock did a 2 for 1 split in March 1999 and soared more than 50 percent in the eighteen months following. In the 1999 Shareholder letter Warren Buffet had to swallow down a McCrow. "My decision to sell McDonalds was a very big mistake," Buffet wrote. "Overall, you would have been better off last year If I had regularly shucked off to the movies during market hours."

The reality is: no one is infallible. We all make mistakes. Even professionals and experts make mistakes. What distinguishes the men from the boys and the women from the girls, is how we react to the mistake. And what we do to take corrective action. When your Financial Advisor makes a mistake — and this is a likelihood in the real world where no one is perfect — don't panic. Watch how they handle the mistake. In most cases, you will gain a valuable insight into their level of professionalism. The most important thing to do when a mistake happens is to respond with appropriate and corrective action.

"The future comes one day at a time."

—Abraham Lincoln

203

Chapter 8 Review

- There is a difference between investing and gambling. A big difference.

- The Investment Rules Are:

  a) Have a plan.

  b) Don't put all your eggs in one basket.

  c) Don't fiddle with your funds.

  d) The market will reward companies that make money.

- Everyone makes mistakes.

- Mistakes can be wonderful opportunities.

- Our attitude effects our ability to deal with mistakes.

- How to Handle a Mistake:

    1. Admit it and accept it.

    2. Keep your eye on the ball.

    3. Learn from it, and forget about who is to blame.

    4. Reach for each other.

    5. Be gentle with yourself.

    6. Control the damage.

    7. Focus on what is going right.

    8. Never hesitate to seek help.

Chapter Nine

☙

The Value of a Financial Advisor

Chapter Nine

The Value of a Financial Advisor

*"There is a world of difference
between a good sound investment,
and an investment that sounds good."*
—Anonymous

In looking back on my career, my clients made the most money when I did something that I was never paid to do — I convinced them not to sell. I can not begin to count the number of times I persuaded clients to hold on to stocks or mutual funds, to their eventual and substantial gain. In a nutshell, that is the role and the value of a good Financial Advisor.

With the advent of the internet, too many investors began treating their portfolios like interactive computer games. Advertising campaigns targeted such investors and sent them the message that it would be easy, fun and could be oh-so-profitable to "do it yourself."

"You're gonna hate online trading. Add that to the list of things my broker was wrong about," captioned one ad. *"I had a stock broker for the better part of 10 years. The only one who is broker is me,"* chided another. While it may be true that internet investing is cheap, there is one economic law that can never be revoked: You get what you pay for.

> *"He who is always his own counselor will often have a fool for his client."*
>
> —Anonymous

I guess it is expected that someone in my position would have that opinion, but it is only because I know this business. I know how complex it is, how volatile it can be, and I know what's at stake. I live, breath, walk and talk this business. I also know how humbling it can be.

If you are like most people, your interest in the financial world — no matter how avid — is not your passion. If it were, you'd likely be in this business. But it need not be your passion for you to be a successful investor. The key to financial success lies in the ability to simplify the financial planning process, and obtain the guidance of a financial professional.

The financial services industry has experienced dramatic change in recent years and many investment firms and advisors have launched a new way to do business. They are moving away from a transaction fee structure to an annual fee based on the total dollar amount of client assets. Clients pay a simple annual fee based on the value of their assets. In return, they receive unlimited trading with the advice and guidance of a professional.

This new approach aligns the client's goals with the Financial Advisor. Both want to increase the value of the account. If the account goes up, the Financial Advisor makes more money. If the account goes down, the Financial Advisor makes less money. It's that simple. The Financial Advisor now sits on the same side of the desk as the client. It's about time.

If investment research, analysis and selection are your gummy bears or cup of tea, then the world of e-trading is for you. The pace is lickety-split, and once you're good (this takes time, like any specialized skill) you might even match market performance. My position on day trading for the average person is that it should not exceed your gambling budget. In other words, use whatever amount of funds you would be comfortable dropping at a table in Las Vegas. Investment portfolios and retirement nest eggs should not be handled in this manner. Just because you make tons of trades doesn't mean you are an investor, any more than having 1000 one-night-stands means you are a romantic.

Earn Higher Returns with a Financial Advisor

Investors who use a financial advisor earn higher returns than direct-market investors, according to a lengthy and thorough study by the respected fund measurement firm DALBAR, Inc.

For the period used for the study (March 1990 to December 1999), the comparative return for the Morgan Stanley World index, which was used as a proxy for the typical foreign equity fund, rose a total of 313 percent. On a compound annual basis, the average investor's return was only 7.34 percent compared with 15.52 percent annually for the world index. Cumulative returns were higher on equity funds (114 percent versus 98 percent) and on income funds (162 percent versus 131 percent).

In looking at past studies of investor behavior done in the U.S. by DALBAR, Inc. dating back to 1994, we find that clients of financial advisors had generally higher returns. Is this because they were encouraged to stay invested through good times and bad?

Clearly, facts indicate investors who use a financial professional (and listen to their advice!) do much better than those who do not. Please remember this the next time persuasive advertising tempts you to strike out on your own, or switch from one fund to another. Keep in mind, it is only advertising.

How to Maximize Your Relationship With Your Financial Advisor

The relationship with your financial advisor is an important one. You already know this. But did you know that you may be inadvertently "shooting yourself in the foot" by how you interact with him/her? You can make the relationship better by following these tips.

1. Allow your Advisor to do his/her job.

To a Financial Advisor, the profile of their 'best' clients are people who allow them to do their jobs. The 'best' clients are the ones who listen and take advice. This is, after all, what you are paying for. Clients who constantly second guess their Financial Advisor do not make the best client list. All Financial Advisors make recommendations to their clients. But the clients must follow these recommendations for them to do any good. You must have the ability to delegate, and allow your Financial Advisor to do his/her job.

I always told my clients right from the beginning that I was there to "drive the bus." I was confident in my ability to get them from A to B faster and more efficiently than they could on their own, but they had to let me do my job. If mistakes happened (as they sometimes do), I told them that we would then be proactive and get back on the road to their final destination. I told them that if all they could give me was 10 percent of their trust, I would earn the other 90 percent, but it all hinged on their ability to follow my lead.

Why do 'best' clients make the most money? It is human nature. Best clients get phoned first. The clients who resist allowing the Financial Advisor to do their jobs get called last (and by then the opportunity might be over.)

2. Be honest, and give your Financial Advisor the full picture.

Be absolutely honest with your Financial Advisor regarding your risk tolerance. He or she won't think any more of you if your risk tolerance is high. At the same time, they will not think less of you if your risk tolerance is low. They just want to accurately know what it is, so they can match you with the best investments according to your needs, goals and risk tolerance.

Some misguided investors overstate their risk tolerance and then expect their Financial Advisor to be their emotional babysitter or hand-holder every time the market hiccups. None of us mind doing a bit of this. But we draw the line when you put us on speed dial and call us daily just to hear us tell you "everything is okay." This takes away from the time we need to do what it is that we do so well. An overstated risk tolerance at the beginning of the relationship is not in your best interest. Know yourself well enough to communicate an appropriate risk level. Please.

And be straightforward regarding your other investments. Your Financial Advisor needs the whole picture to do the best job for you. I never minded when a new client set up an account with me that was only a portion of their entire investments, as long as I knew what the others were. Many times, investors wanted to see what I could do with a portion before they gave me their entire investment portfolio. I understand.

Bring a copy of your statements from all your other investment firms. Your Financial Advisor needs the whole picture if you want him/her to give you the best advice. He or she will appreciate you even more if you say something like, "Here's a copy of our other statements, so you can keep these in mind while you are putting a portfolio together for us." That way, duplication can be avoided, and you will get a better investment recommendation.

3.   Do not confuse motion with progress.

I will probably always remember Mr. Barrington. He came in to my office one day with some uncomfortable news. He was leaving me, he said. He was moving his account somewhere else.

For nearly two hours, I endeavored to find out why he would want to leave. I needed to know what had prompted him to feel that way. How could it be? Especially after exceeding his expected returns and service for six years. If my office dropped the ball somewhere, I had to know. I am always interested in knowing what could be done better.

Was it the service? No, Mr. Barrington assured me he was very pleased with it. Was he unhappy with his portfolio? NO, he said he had always been more than happy with my recommendations. Then what was it?

He kept reassuring me that he was entirely happy with my office, and even said that he was going to miss me. He insisted he really liked me, my staff, and that everything was fine. But I couldn't leave it at that. I figure there's no way a guy gets up in the morning and decides to move $750,000 for no reason. There *had* to be a reason. I pressed for the answer.

"Well, Ken," he said, "I just don't know why. There's nothing the new firm can do for me that you aren't already doing. I know that. The best way I can describe it is like this — it's like walking down the street and seeing some shoes in the window. I don't need any shoes. I have a closet full of them. But I look at them and think, geez, it would be nice to have a new pair of shoes...."

For a moment I was speechless, and those who know me can vouch those moments are rare. But I was speechless because I could barely believe what I had just heard. Changing Financial Advisors because you want the feeling of a new pair of shoes? Where, oh where, is the logic here? Mr. Barrington would have been much better off, had he gone out and bought himself that new pair of shoes he wanted.

There's something mysterious that happens to many investors around the five year mark with their advisors. I've heard it called The Five Year Itch, and it happens in relationships and marriages. There is a phase around this time that a certain restlessness sets in, or an "itch." If left alone, it will go away without scratching. What amazes me is that Mr. Barrington was the only one who came in and told me directly.

I respect Mr. Barrington for telling me to my face. Usually, a Financial Advisor finds out about these things via an internal office memo, which we find a little rude. But I still think he should have gone to his medicine cabinet for some Calamine lotion and applied it to his "itch." He should have taken a bath in it, if necessary. There is no doubt in my mind it would have been better for him.

Because it is the client who loses. With any switch-for-no-good reason movement of funds, someone other than the client benefits. I can tell you the first thing that is likely to happen to Mr. Barrington's portfolio is the new advisor will want to change it. Much like a male dog likes to tag his area, the new advisor will want to make his/her mark. The timing is often poor, and the client inevitably loses. The new advisor will sell high quality equities or companies and replace them with a different mix of high quality equities or companies (the ones that he/she follows).

Shuffling the deck just to shuffle the deck is not in an investor's best interest. Whatever compounding there was, will be lost. And then there is the capital gain tax expense. The advisor may gain commissions and a new client, but it is very unlikely the client will benefit in an end analysis.

If your Financial Advisor is providing a level of service that you are happy with, and is on top of your goals (and achieving them) resist the impulse to change. Changing advisors simply for the sake of change is silly. Do not confuse motion with progress. A rocking horse can move like crazy, but it never makes any headway. Remember that.

The Right Questions to Ask

During my 16 year period in the business, I was asked about references by potential new clients only twice. I mentioned this in conversation to a colleague and she reacted with flat out disbelief.

I understood her incredulity. Who hires a new housekeeper, babysitter, handyman, or whatever without grilling for references? It's usually one of the first things we think of asking. But not, apparently, when it comes to our Financial Advisors. She still couldn't believe it.

"That has to be peculiar to you," she said. "I bet other advisors get asked for references all the time."

I knew they didn't, but just to prove my point I phoned two fellow Financial Advisors while she sat and listened. The first one has been in the business 12 years.

"How many times have you been asked for references?" I asked him.

"Never!" was his reply.

I quickly called another friend, who has been in the business 20 years, and asked him the same question. His answer was three times. Between the three of us, there is nearly 50 years of business practice. Yet between the three of us, with the hundreds of new clients we've seen, only five thought to ask for references. That always amazed me.

It's my experience that new clients rarely ask the right questions. They almost always ask, "Where's the market going?" All the questions in an typical initial appointment are related to products, individual stocks, mutual funds and market decisions. These may be good questions for a second meeting (IF there is a second meeting).

Here's my suggestions for some better questions to ask:

- How many firms have you been with?

- How much longer are you planning to be in the business?

- What level of service can I expect?

- How many clients do you have?

- What is your average account size?

- Will I be dealing with you, or one of your associates?

- What's your ideal client?

- What do your monthly statements look like?

- What is in *your* investment portfolio?

I'll show you mine, if you show me yours.

Personally, if it were me, I would always ask the last question. It's important to ask for credentials and inquire about their training, but you can learn more about a Financial Advisor by looking at his/her portfolio.

It is a way to find out if the Financial Advisor is realistic or just blowing smoke, if you know what I mean. Don't forget, Financial Advisors are highly trained in the art of persuasion. (If we were all so good at picking stocks, we'd all be professional money managers!)

If you ask to see his/her portfolio statement, you can find out if they "practice what they preach." It is always a good sign if they do. Wouldn't you get a little apprehensive if you were on a Ford car lot and the salesperson (trying to sell you a Ford) drives a Toyota? Of course you would. If I had a Financial Advisor who was telling me to do one thing, while he/she was personally doing something quite different, I would find another advisor.

A final question I would be sure to ask is, "How will you monitor performance and report the progress?" Our industry is notorious for doing a brutally poor job of producing clear, understandable reports. As a client so eloquently said, "Ken, when I get my statement, I go directly to the last page. I only care about the number in the bottom right hand corner. The rest is just noise."

As an investor, here's what you will want to know:

- How much money went in?

- How much money went out?

- What is my return, in dollars and cents?

- What's my percentage return, and what is my return annualized?

- What's my return, on an annualized basis since we've been together?

Find out how the Financial Advisor does his/her performance reporting *before* you begin the relationship. Make sure you will get the information you want in a way that makes sense to you. Clearly, and easily.

I urge you to ask the right questions and find the right Financial Advisor for you. Then stick with him or her. Take the time to build the relationship, just like you take the time to build anything worthwhile. Based on honesty and trust, a good relationship can be a rewarding experience.

Never more true than when it comes to your Financial Advisor.

Behind the Scenes

Ever wonder what your Financial Advisor does once you leave the office after your appointment? Think he/she puts their feet up on the desk and placidly waits for the next appointment? Not in my experience!

PICKING STOCKS

Lee Iaccoca's principle — *You either lead, follow or get out of the way* — applies when it comes to picking stocks. It is virtually impossible for the average person to lead, as that requires a direct pipeline to management. However, with the guidance of a Financial Advisor, one can do a damn good job of following Mining the gossip at a cocktail party is no substitute for a Financial Advisor with an informed opinion. Here's how facts are gathered:

1. Research.

Most Financial Advisors are voracious readers. They make notes of the companies being recommended and look for overlap. For example, does Morgan Stanley Dean Witter have the same rating for a company as Merrill Lynch? Or is it different?

There is an abundance of information on the internet, which can lead people to believe they can do a good job of their own research. But while information is plentiful, judgment is scarce. It is much easier for a Financial Advisor, who has a "finger on the pulse," to get a more accurate feel for the general consensus of opinions and recommendations. This is their job. Even the newbie financial professional listens to the same daily conference call as the seasoned veteran, and participates in the boardroom conversations when the fund managers visit.

2. Observe what the professional money managers are buying.

It is possible for the average person to use monthly, quarterly and annual reports to look for money managers' top selections. And mutual fund tracking programs such as PalTrak or Morning Star are great for finding out what the professionals are buying. But the problem is that by the time this information is posted, it is old news to those inside the industry. Financial Advisors have this information first, and this is an industry where time is of the essence.

They also keep a watchful eye for continuity between managers, and situations where research analysts agree with the money managers. If they notice that Merrill Lynch, for example, has buy recommendations on the same stock that professional money managers are buying, the stock is definitely worth looking at.

3. Monitor what insiders are buying and selling.

It is important to find out why insiders are selling. If senior management is buying back their own shares, this is a strong commitment that they are trying to maximize shareholder value. You can get this information from financial publications, business magazines and the internet. But, you must read the newspapers daily and diligently. This information is easy to miss.

Often when companies have cash available to make acquisitions, fund R&D (Research & Development), or enhance their technology, they sometimes view buying back their shares as the best investment for their cash. This is another strong buying signal that a Financial Advisor can quickly recognize.

There is more to picking stocks than just knowing a company's name.

One of Peter Lynch's mottos is: *buy companies that you understand.* It is a good one. There are far too many people independently buying stocks in companies that they don't understand. Worse, they don't even know what the company does!

People, listen to me, please. If you do not understand what the company does, and you can't name two of their competitors, then you are clearly gambling. Gambling is not investing. For goodness sake, forget about what your friends, neighbors or relatives are buying. Learn to rely on your Financial Advisor to keep you in the investment arena.

MUTUAL FUNDS

The mutual fund business today can be best described as marketing warfare. With the entry of the Boomer gang into the marketplace, competition became, and remains fierce among mutual funds. Marketing departments everywhere were summoned, and continue to work overtime.

223

Their messages are everywhere they think you might be looking or listening. Buy this fund! Now you need this fund! And the latest and greatest is this fund! Wait a second, now there is this fund and you had better buy this one too! Sound familiar? Marketing is an energetic business, isn't it?

There are now more mutual funds in the United States than there are stocks on the New York Stock Exchange. There are only 2,785* companies listed on the NYSE, but there are 11,287* mutual funds. In Canada there are even more (3,207*) funds per capita than in the United States. Folks, this is nuts. It has become virtually impossible for investors and financial advisors to keep up with the latest craze or more specifically, the mutual fund flavor of the month.

There are sector funds, environmental funds, medical funds, technology, telecom, real estate, biotech, consumer products, leisure and recreation, entertainment and communications, precious metals, and financial services funds. The list grows almost daily and the information to keep abreast of all of them is overwhelming, if not impossible.

If you have the time and the inclination, it is good to read, research and familiarize yourself with the marketplace. But let the advice and recommendations of your Financial Advisor carry the most weight in your decision-making regarding mutual fund selections. They are in the best position. Not only to weed through the information, but to benefit from their direct contact with fund managers, who often make the office rounds. There

* Figures as of April 30, 2000.

is no substitute for being able to 'grill' or simply question the fund managers or their representatives directly, which only a Financial Advisor can.

One should always consider that the "s" in RRSP stands for "savings" and not "speculation" and the "R" in IRA stands for "Retirement" and not "Risk."

Mutual Fund Mistakes

One of the first things a Financial Advisor does with a new client's investment portfolio is to check for some common mutual fund mistakes. If you have been an independent investor up until now, you may be inadvertently making one (or more!) of them. If you have *any* concerns after reading this section, make an appointment with a Financial Advisor to help you rectify the situation. That's what they do.

The Most Common Mutual Fund Mistake is...

The most common mutual fund mistake is over diversification. Some of us in the industry refer to it as "diworsification." It means too few dollars are being spread out over far too many funds. When you remember the energetic marketing efforts of the sponsoring companies, it is easy to understand why this happens so often.

Take Harold C., for example. His portfolio value is $190,000 averaging approximately $12,000 in each fund.

That means he has 15 or 16 different funds. Harold thinks he's doing a good thing by buying lots of different funds. But well-intentioned as he may be, Harold is making a mistake.

In reality, his portfolio would be much more efficient with just four funds, with an average of approximately $48,000 in each. Why? The average portfolio manager holds approximately 40 to 60 names in a portfolio. With a portfolio of 200 stocks, that is more diversification than you need. Eight hundred companies is clearly an overkill!

What role do advertising and marketing play in Harold's thinking? I've wondered. The best marketers simply find out what it is that people want to hear, and then find a way to send that message. And they can be devious! Not only do they find a way to tell people what they want to hear, but they do it in a way that is hard to criticize. Marketing is not a new business. These folks have had decades of experience.

Back in the 1950s an advertisement submitted to *The New York Times* with the wording "naughty but nice" had it changed to "Paris-inspired — but so nice." And a nightclub advertisement of "50 of the hottest girls this side of hell" became "50 of the most alluring maidens this side of paradise." Same message, just reworded to pass scrutiny.

So if you feel like the fund ads are speaking to you, and saying just the right things — they probably are! But temper your reaction with the knowledge that it is a premeditated campaign, using some of the cleverest minds available. Don't succumb to every message. You don't need a zillion funds. Stay the course and stick to your plan with your Financial Advisor.

The Second Most Common Mutual Fund Mistake

The second most common mistake is chasing last year's winners. Again, think marketing and advertising. Many investors get blind-sided by the numbers and messages couched in marketing materials. It's like standing in front of a moving freight train.

The best performing funds are always the ones picked for advertising and marketing purposes. But past performance is not a guarantee of future results. Forget about chasing last years winners and buying the hot funds *after* they've been hot.

Typically, funds with the largest redemptions are big successful funds that are temporarily out of favor. A good Financial Advisor knows that last year's dogs, or unpopular funds, can be a better alternative.

In the United States, investors pulled about $5.8 billion more money out of Brandywine in 1998 than they put in. Manager Foster Friess made several wrong moves that year, and the fund fell 0.7 percent. This, by itself is not bad. But when you consider the S&P 500 did 34 percent that year, it was very bad. The opportunity cost is always a factor. But he recovered nicely the next year — the fund was up 49.9 percent. I see the same thing happen in Canada. The Templeton Growth Fund only did 0.7 percent in 1998 but it posted a strong 21.1 percent in 1999.

Do your research but resist the temptations offered by clever marketing. Listen to what your Financial Advisor has to say.

The Third Most Common Mutual Fund Mistake

The third most common mistake is the duplication of funds with the same style and the same stocks. There is no point in owning two American growth funds that all have Microsoft, General Electric, Cisco Systems, MCI World Inc., AT&T Corp and Lucent Technology. There's no point to it, but without the benefit of a good Financial Advisor's counsel, many people make this mistake without realizing it.

If you check among the biggest and most well known funds and look at their top 10 stocks, you will see similar names. Why own two of those funds? The situation is similar in Canada. There is no point in owning two Canadian growth funds as you will see the same names in each. The Royal Bank, Bank of Montreal, Nortel, BCE Inc., Imperial Oil, Suncor Energy Inc. and Bombardier are in both portfolios. The duplication serves no purpose.

A good Financial Advisor knows this, and will help you achieve a balance between Growth and Value managed funds. That's what they do. Financial Advisors recognize that despite the endless analysis of which style is better, in reality a fairly simple truth exists:

Value managers tend to outperform in bear markets, and Growth managers tend to outperform in bull markets.

Many Financial Advisors share my belief that it is better to diversify according to management styles than to stick with only one style for a prolonged period of time.

No one holds a crystal ball that predicts market trends. It would be nice if we did, but we don't.

So it has always made sense to me that an investment portfolio be balanced between Growth and Value management styles. For example, if a client had four mutual funds, I would recommend two be with Growth managers and two be with Value style managers.

This strategy also eliminates the critical question of when to switch styles if you have gone totally one way or the other. More than one investor has stuck to one style for a while, even while it was under performing. And just when they've had enough and switched — you guessed it — the fund they abandoned comes back and their new fund drops!

Switching from value to growth or growth to value can be a huge mistake. Timing is everything. Once again, I want to reiterate the importance of having a Financial Advisor's involvement.

Read Between the Books

I can't leave this subject without a comment on the cornucopia of mutual fund books that spill on to the marketplace every year. Each one touts itself as the latest and greatest guidebook.

Have you ever wondered what would happen if someone actually took the advice from these books? Well, a Toronto investment advisor studied the recom- mendations from four of the most popular annual fund books. She compiled four years of recommendations and tracked how the funds did in subsequent years. And here's what she found . . .

Between 47 and 81 percent of the picks in the balanced US and Canadian equity sectors *did worse than the median fund* in their categories. In only 2 cases did she find that the books managed to place more than half of their picks in a category above the median fund.

"You would probably do better if you simply threw darts at a list of mutual funds and bought the one you happen to hit," she concluded.

BONDS

Many investors do not understand that bonds are as equally volatile as stocks. The complexities of the bond market can be underestimated by the average investor, and my advice would be to seek the opinion of a professional. He/she can help you decide what is best for you. It will depend on the expected direction of interest rates and your risk/reward profile.

If you feel compelled to add bonds to your portfolio, then do yourself a favor and buy the real McCoy rather than a bond fund. This is better because it allows you to control the yield curve. And it is substantially more cost effective, as you will not be paying an annual management fee.

If you are a cautious investor with a low risk tolerance, your Financial Advisor might suggest you build a bond ladder, which can be an effective strategy. Take 20 percent and go out for 1 year, 20 percent for 2 years, 20 percent for three years, 20 percent for four years and 20 percent for five years. If you are slightly more aggressive, and don't need access to your capital you may move further out on the yield curve and build a ladder starting at five years. This strategy will take the guess work out of interest rate forecasting.

" When a man has not a good reason for doing a thing...
He has good reason for letting it alone."
—Walter Scott

ASSET ALLOCATION

Asset allocation is the distribution of investment funds among categories of assets such as cash equivalents, stocks, fixed-income investment, and such tangible assets as real estate, precious metals and collectibles.

There are countless studies on the benefits of asset allocation. One conducted by Brinson, Singel and Beebower of 82 large U.S. pension fund managers concluded that successful allocation was responsible for 91.5 percent of overall portfolio returns.

The challenge with asset allocation and strategic asset allocation (strategic allocation is the so-called ability to be able to predict the right time to be in cash, bonds, and/or stocks) is that the best performing asset class is difficult or impossible to identify in advance. No one has a crystal ball here, either. Today's best performing asset class may not be tomorrow's best performer. For investors with a one to five year time line, adhering to an asset allocation philosophy will not necessarily guarantee the highest returns. (It will, however, definitely lessen the impact on a portfolio in a severe market downturn.)

For investors with a time line of upward to 10 years and beyond, my advice would simply be to talk to your Financial Advisor about forgetting asset allocation altogether. Because despite the tremendous volatility in stocks over the last decade, blue chip equities, when held for 10 to 20 years have consistently offered greater growth potential while providing an inflationary hedge.

In his book *Stocks for the Long Run*, Dr. Jeremy J. Siegel looked at various holding periods between 1871 and 1996. Having analyzed each 20-year holding period, he found that stocks outperformed bonds and T-bills 94.4 percent and 99.1 percent of the time, respectively, on an inflation-adjusted basis.

Dr. Jon J Kanitz, Ph.D., contributing editor to *The Money Letter* and Director of Wood Gundy Private Client Investments in Toronto, shares my opinion when he wrote: "Personally... my strategy remains as follows — 100 percent stocks, and 50 percent of that in the Yankee market. This is my idea of a balanced portfolio."

INDEXING

Like the debate over growth investing versus value investing, there will also be a debate over passive management versus active management. The controversy will probably continue for decades to come.

Buying the index looks fantastic when the market goes straight up for an extended period of time, as we have seen in the United States since 1994. It also looks good when a select few companies within the index account for the lion's share of the index's total return.

In 1997, the gain on the TSE 300 was highly concentrated in just seven stocks. Royal Bank, Toronto Dominion Bank, Bank of Nova Scotia, Canadian Imperial Bank of Commerce, Bank of Montreal, Nortel Networks Corp. and BCE Inc. accounted for the bulk of the gain. In 1999, the TSE 300 had a total return (dividends reinvested) of 31.7 percent. However, if you removed Nortel Networks Corp. and BCE Inc. from the index, the advance for the TSE 300 would have been reduced to a mere 6.9 percent. Yikes!

It is very difficult for a portfolio manager to outperform the market when the 1999 return on Nortel was 280 percent and BCE was 126 percent. At the end of December 1999 they accounted for 27 percent of the TSE. The pattern was very similar in the U.S. as 10 stocks in the S&P 500 accounted for the majority of the return.

We all know that markets can't continue to go up forever. I can assure you that indexing in a bear market will be as popular and painful as having your wisdom teeth pulled. For nearly two decades, I have been steadfast in my belief, and I will go to my deathbed believing the human element adds value at the end of the day in the long run. Indexing can't replace a good relationship with a Financial Advisor.

MARKET TIMING

The theory of market timing is to sell stocks or equity funds near a market top, remain in cash during a bear market, and near the end — ideally just before the next bull roars and the market takes off again — reinvest the cash in stocks and equity funds. Pardon me for a minute while I take a deep breath after that sentence. I don't blame you if you want to do the same. It was quite a mouthful.

Frankly, it's a mouthful that I have a hard time swallowing.

It would take a crystal ball to engage in perfect market timing. I don't care who you are, unless you are God Himself, it is virtually impossible to consistently anticipate what the market is going to do next. The dangers of market timing and the pitfalls of being incorrect are severe.

In 1998, for example, the S&P 500 Index was up 28.6 percent for the entire year. However, investors who missed the best 10 trading days would have seen their portfolios drop by 6 percent for the year. A 17-year study by Charles Kade *"Dow 10,000 — Fact or Fiction,"* showed that investors who missed the best 30 trading days out of nearly 4,400 would have seen a 9 percent return versus 21 percent. Their return would be cut by more than half.

In another study by Ibbotson Associates, hypothetical research indicates the value of $1.00 invested in 1925 would have grown to $2351 by 1998 (assuming reinvestment of income and no transaction costs or taxes, and based on the S&P 500 Index). During that 73 year time frame, there were 876 months. If you missed the best 40 months, which is a mere 4.5 percent of the time, your $2351.00 value would have tumbled to a dismal $14.10.

A Word About Market Timing

Market	Index	Fully Invested	Missed Best 10	Missed Best 20	Missed Best 30	Missed Best 40
UK	All Share	16.2%	12.8%	10.5%	8.5%	6.7%
USA	S&P 500	19.1%	15.4%	12.7%	10.4%	8.3%
Germany	DAX 30	17.5%	11.9%	8.2%	5.3%	2.7%
France	CAC40	19.4%	14.8%	11.4%	8.5%	6.1%

All figures show annualized, total returns, from 31 December 1987 to 31 December 1999, in local currency terms.

BUY AND HOLD

Buy and hold is a valid strategy, but it is one that investors today seem to ignore. The Nasdaq Index has been turning over its shares at three times the pace of any other major industrialized market in the world. In the United States in 1999, investors held stocks for just over 8 months on average. A decade ago, the average holding period was two years.

And trading activity has been of epidemic proportion in the dot com world. The average holding period for Amazon.com shares at one point was seven days. The average holding period was only five days for DoubleClick and a mere 72 hours for Priceline.com. Everyone was trying to be a market timing genius!

Study after study continues to support that it is better to be a market participant than a market timer. Buy and hold does not mean buy, hold and ignore. It means buy, hold, monitor (with your Financial Advisor) and be proactive when necessary.

Investor Psychology

The major difficulty within a buy and hold strategy is being able to handle the emotional side of investing, especially when we go through periods of volatility. The psychology of the market is very powerful.

Since 1890, the market has had seven notable downturns followed by periods of bear conditions. The last downturn occurred in 1987, but recovery occurred within two years. That's a very quick recovery. Compare it to 1929, when the market fell 89 percent. Recovery took 26 years! The average period for recovery after a downturn is 11 years, as shown by the following table. The average decline is 57 percent.

Peak Year	% decline	Years to recovery
1890	64	15
1906	64	10
1916	56	9
1929	89	26
1966	38	7
1973	45	10
1987	42	2
Average	**57**	**11**

Buy and hold strategies are very hard to maintain during down periods. They are usually abandoned, and replaced with "sell at all costs." It has been a long time since there has been a prolonged bear market. The last one was in 1973, so most investors today (or money managers, for that matter!) have no experience with bear conditions. We've never had to be patient. We forget that the Nifty Fifty stocks took many, many years to recover from the 1973 downturn. Check out the next table, and imagine yourself as an investor in the market during the long, slow climb back.

Nifty Fifty Then and Now

1973	1/5/73 Share Price	12/6/74 Share Price	% drop	Years to Regain 1973 High
General Electric	$4.59	$2.10	-54.25	9.5
Cocoa-Cola	$3.01	$0.95	-68.44	12.3
Disney	$2.30	$0.38	-83.48	12.9
IBM	$41.89	$20.56	-50.92	9.8
Eastman Kodak	$66.15	$26.50	-59.94	14.5
Xerox	$50.50	$18.17	-64.02	23.3
Avon	$67.25	$14.19	-78.90	24.5
Johnson&Johnson	$5.36	$3.29	-38.62	9.5
Polaroid	$62.81	$9.44	-84.97	Not yet
McDonald's	$3.65	$1.49	-59.18	9.5
S&P 500	120	65	-45.77	7.5

Psychologically, it is easier to be an investor when the market is going straight up, as it did from 1994 through the end of the century. But imagine being an investor when the market is in a downward spiral and threatening to collapse in front of your eyes. Who is to say it won't happen again?

I think the single most important message in regarding investor psychology in the new millennium is to lower expectations on returns. The high double digit returns are passe. I will not be the least bit surprised if rates of return fall back more in line with historical averages. So I recommend using a realistic number of 10 percent to 12 percent when making your projections. Many people are still expecting at least 20 percent returns, and beyond. That's just not tenable going forward, in my opinion.

But my experience is that you just can't tell some people. They won't listen. They seem to think that what is being stated applies to everyone else, but not to them. Do you know people like that?

I know that doctors experience a similar frustration with it, and they refer to it as 'patient compliance.' The difference is that with doctors, the more serious the illness, the higher the patient's compliance.

When you are really ill, the chances of you doing exactly what the doctor tells you to do is high. As patients get better, they are less inclined to take the doctor's prescribed regimen seriously. Patient compliance drops. They will listen, nod their heads and then completely ignore the advice altogether. Doctors find this behavior frustrating. So do Financial Advisors. Like the doctor telling you to do what he thinks will benefit you, Financial Advisors tell you what they believe will help your portfolio.

But you can't be helped unless you can take advice. Working out a realistic financial plan, and staying the course takes a Financial Advisor's involvement. He/she will guide you through the emotions and reactions of market changes. In the process, he/she will help you react logically and rationally rather than spontaneously and irrationally. Yogi Berra said it so well...

"90% of the game is half mental."

Chapter 9 Review

- There is a world of difference between a good sound investment, and an investment that sounds good.

- The key to financial success lies in the ability to simplify the financial planning process, and obtain the guidance of a financial professional.

- Three things that can improve the relationship with a Financial Advisor are:

    1. Allow them to do their job, and take their advice.

    2. Be honest, and give the full picture.

    3. Understand that motion is not always progress.

- People who work with a Financial Advisor earn higher returns on their investment portfolios than those who try and do it on their own.

Chapter Ten

And Then What?

Chapter Ten

And Then What?

*"Life itself can't give you joy,
Unless you really will it;
Life just gives you time and space—
It's up to you to fill it."*

—Anonymous

Anybody who thinks that enough money will make them happy should meet John and Marcy. They ought to be one of the happiest couples in the world. They have two grown sons to be proud of, every material asset and trinket they could want, and a financial freedom that few people experience.

John and Marcy became wealthy when they were quite young, with a few million inherited dollars. Shortly after, the European stock market took a fortunate swing for them. Their few million very quickly became $19 million. If money was all it took for happiness, John and Marcy would be euphoric. But in truth, they aren't. Happiness eludes them, and neither John nor Marcy know why.

They try hard, really hard to make themselves happy. Marcy relentlessly shops for it in designer boutiques and "by appointment only" stores. She hasn't found it yet, but a trail of platinum credit card receipts attest to her diligent efforts.

John is no slouch in his pursuit of happiness, either. He regularly consults with his personal chef to come up with the ultimate in gourmet indulgences. This is all very much to the delight of guests invited to the lavish evenings, but it has no lasting effect on John. He wakes up just as bored the next morning as he was the day before. He tries to appease himself with frequent golf games, but they often are more frustrating than fun.

Poor John and Marcy. They have it all, but they are not content. There is no peace of mind in their household. Life is not happy for either of them. Too bad they didn't hear a wise old gentleman's diagnosis of their plight.

"How sad," he said, as he watched them one day. "They have no purpose."

I think the old guy nailed it. Beyond a good golf score and another hunt for the latest designer labels, John and Marcy have no reason to get up in the morning. They are rich as kings with money. But they are poor as paupers when it comes to purpose. They use their energy and considerable finances for little else beyond catering to their own personal desires and wishes. Pampering yourself may feel great for a while, but without something of interest beyond oneself, life inevitably becomes dull. Without purpose, life is empty.

When is enough, enough?

How much is enough? Without a grip on how much is enough, we can become caught in a frenzy of consumerism, and our life becomes vainly about lavishing ourselves with 'toys.' At some point, we should all ask ourselves how much is enough. We need to know the answer. Because if we don't, we might keep running past the goal posts. And if we do that, we will eventually hit the wall. When we hit the wall, we splatter.

We all know examples of successful zillionaires who are still the first to get to the office each morning and the last to leave each day. How much money will ever be enough? Has working become so much of a habit? Or is it, as some have suggested, an addiction to work? Power?

I have often wondered what drives people past the point of reason or balance. Most of us also know examples of people like John and Marcy. Maybe they don't have as much money as John and Marcy, but the behavior is archetypical of people without purpose.

Once you have reached whatever is your "magical nut," and acquired enough money to live comfortably as you wish, then what? At some point you have to stop being a consumer, and realize that what you have is enough. (And maybe that what you have is pretty wonderful.) If you already have your ideal cottage in the Muskokas, do you really need another one in Florida? And then what? Will you then need another one in the Hamptons? And then what? Where does it end?

Perhaps the inability to answer the "and then what" question explains why suddenly 'coming into a bunch of money,' or winning the lottery is devastating for many people. You would be amazed at the number of people who win a lottery and are miserable, broke, or broke *and* miserable 10 years later. Money did not solve all their problems. They had no plan after the big win, or newly acquired financial freedom. There was no sense of purpose in their lives. And that is sad.

A person without a purpose is like a boat without a rudder. Money alone does not define the man or woman. Neither the abundance, nor lack of it, distinguishes the true quality of a person's life. That is determined by our sense of purpose, or what *meaning* life has for us. And what we *do* with it.

*"A man's character can be defined
by what he is worth if he lost all his money."*
—Anonymous

Now What?

Our sense of purpose, meaning, or reason for life is important. We need it at every stage of life. And as we go through different stages in life, we might find ourselves in the position of needing a new purpose. Retirement is certainly one of the stages of change. Reaching success is another one.

Consider the personal experience of Henry B. Roy, chairman of the executive committee of Roy & Crown, one of the largest public relations firms. Henry, at a high point in his career, got out of bed one morning and shuddered at the prospect of going to work. Suddenly, after years of enjoyment, he felt little gratification for his accomplishments.

"Is this all there is?' he asked himself.

For years, Henry had dedicated himself to becoming a top executive in his field of work. He had a clear purpose and with his talent and determination, he was set for success. But he had never taken the time to determine what success meant to him, or what would happen once he achieved it. So when he reached the goal post he just kept running. He stopped before he realized he didn't have the vaguest idea of where he was heading. In short, he lacked a purpose at that stage of his life. Sometimes the reality of success doesn't always match the dream of success. Henry had reached a major goal and it was time for him to create a new one.

Once you've achieved your goal and reached the top of that mountain you were struggling to climb, take this tip from Henry B. Roy: Find another mountain to climb.

Life is a Balancing Act

I always worked hard for my clients, and made time for them when they had something on their mind they wished to discuss or simply share with me. Over the years, I've learned so much from them.

One unforgettable conversation was with Richard D., a retired bank manager. He'd been in to see me for his annual portfolio review. It had been doing quite nicely, but Richard didn't seem as pleased as he could have. I suspected it was because he was still aching from the loss of his wife. She died shortly after he retired. They never had the chance to do all the things they had planned together. The responsibility of his position and his lengthy workdays had kept him away from his wife and family for years. Now that he finally had all the time and money to proceed with their plans, she was gone.

I could tell it was something he deeply regretted. If he had known, would he have spent as much time at the office as he did? Probably not. But at the time, he did not have the luxury of hindsight. I'll always remember his sad words: *"I spent all those years accumulating this stuff, and now I don't have anyone to share it with. And Ken, that's the hardest thing..."*

A Key to Life is Balance

We pay a price, sooner or later, when we cut off areas of our life, or neglect them. Our career, or our pursuit of material wealth is not meant to consume us. Our purpose, or mission in life, is not meant to become an epitome at the cost of everything else, either. Nothing can. Because life is a balancing act. To master life, we must master the art of the balancing four elemental components of a full life.

The four elements are:

1. Physical

2. Emotional

3. Spiritual

4. Mental

Each of the four components — physical, emotional, spiritual and mental — performs a function similar to the four legs of a chair. If your entire life revolves around one single element, your life will have no balance. Think about how much balance there would be if you removed three legs from your chair. If you have one single focus, to the exclusion of everything else, balance will elude you. As a result, so will peace of mind.

Living with only one, two, or three of the above elements in your life will not result in a balanced life. One leg does not make a chair. For a stable chair, there must be four legs. For balance in life, all four elements require your attention.

I have found that it isn't hard to tell when one or more legs are being neglected in my life. It's quite simple — without balance, there is no peace of mind. When I have placed too much emphasis on one element to the detriment of others, it isn't long before I know. Things just don't feel right. I am not at peace with myself. I have learned to listen to the voices of discontent within myself. They are my signal that something is out of balance. It will pester me until I do something about it.

Pest: a thing that is harmful or injurious to man.

When I am feeling that something is not quite right, or out of balance, I take something that a friend developed called The Pest Test. I review each of the four elements and reflect on the role and emphasis they currently hold in my life. If I am honest with myself, what is needed to restore my balance is usually obvious by the time I've completed the review.

THE PEST TEST

P -   Physical

E -   Emotional

S -   Spiritual

T -   Thinking

Physical

When reflecting on the physical aspects of my life, I consider those things that I can touch, hold, feel, hear or see. They are the tangibles. It includes the basics of food, shelter and clothing, as well as the physical body. I ask myself if I am directing too much, or too little energy toward any of the physical areas of my life.

An obsession with material possessions, or an addiction to accumulating them, will surely throw anyone's life off balance. Reliance on material accumulations for a sense of happiness and well-being is just not possible. It will not matter how hard you try, your expectations will not be met. That's because there is more, much more to life than that the things which you own or possess.

> *"If you can't be happy with what you have,*
> *you can't be happy with what you want."*
> —Author Unknown

I can't talk about the physical element without mentioning the e-word. The one I have in mind has nothing to do with the internet, or e-commerce. I mean exercise.

Exercise is a vital part of a good health program, and essential to a balanced life. All we have talked about in this book is meaningless without good health. You know this. Protect your health by doing what you already know you should be doing. If you don't, your life will be out of balance. We need the right foods and we need to be physically active. We need to use our muscles. Remember — if you don't use it, you will lose it.

Physical activity doubles as my antidote for stress. Fortunately for me, a fitness regimen has always been part of my life. It really helped me deal with the stress of my business, which is significant. I've seen the wear and tear effects of 10 to 12 hour days, and burning the candle at both ends. Without the physical activities — workouts, tennis, golf, and cycling—I would not have fared as well as I did. It truly helped me manage stress, and bring balance into my life. You will not find the time to do this. You must *make time* for it, I have learned.

Emotional

The emotional balance in your life comes from interacting with the people you love, and with your friends. Through these relationships we can feel wanted, loved, valued and a sense of belonging. All of these are essential to a state of well being.

Relationships require time, effort and participation. It is easy to "get too busy" and neglect the importance of these relationships. But if we neglect them for long, we will notice that something is missing in our lives. Often it is the richness of relationships with our family and our friends. It is something that money can not buy.

Maintaining good relationships keeps our giving spirit alive. Perhaps herein lies the value of relationships in a balanced life. We receive abundantly in relationships with our family and friends. But unless we reciprocate, and give back, the relationships will deteriorate. Left long enough, they can wither and die. To be alive, relationships require the ebb and flow; the give and take.

"You make a living with what you get,
you make a life by what you give."
—Author Unknown

Not only do our relationships with friends and family keep our giving natures alive, they are a forum for fun. Activities and times that are just pure, simple fun help counteract the serious, stressful effects of responsibilities and careers. Having fun is important. We need to make time for it.

Spiritual

Spirituality is intensely personal. It is what describes the magic in your life, inspires you, fills you with awe and marvel. I like to call it in-spirational, or whatever inspires your spirit. Spiritual nourishment is essential. If it is neglected, your life will not feel balanced.

I enjoy reading stories that inspire. To me, they are as important to read as the financial pages of the newspaper, and I am always on the lookout for them. I never know where I'll find my next one.

In the sports section recently I happened upon a great story about a 17 year old high school student. It really made my day. An only child, Kevin Hall lost his hearing before his third birthday, after contracting H-flu meningitis. Black, young and deaf, Kevin does not consider himself disadvantaged. Instead, he says that he has "wonderful opportunities."

He's already been named junior golfer of the year by the National Minority Golf Foundation, but Kevin has bigger dreams. His goal is to play the PGA Tour. He relishes the chance to be a role model. "I see many African-Americans with no hope and no goals," he says. "I feel if they see a person of their race succeed, they will feel they can do it, too."

"Bad things happen to people," his father said, referring to Kevin's loss of hearing. "We're not always responsible for what happens to us, but we are responsible for how we respond. We chose to respond in a positive way and move forward." I couldn't be more in agreement. It doesn't matter so much what happens to us, it's how we respond that counts.

I find stories like that inspiring. They transcend skin color, age, economic status and geographic borders. They lift my spirits, and give another dimension to my life. I connect with life's goodness.

The best way to ensure the spiritual element is in your life is to have a clear purpose. How are you contributing? How are you making the world a better place? How are you making something better? Who and/or what is better for having crossed your path, or benefited from your involvement?

"We are made wise not by the recollection of our past, but by the responsibility for our future."
—Anonymous

Thoughts

The fourth and final element of a balanced life involves the mental aspect. Your thoughts, and the ongoing stimulation of your mind are also essential for balance in your life.

What new thing have you learned lately? It is never too late to take up a new hobby or a new study. It is important to always keep learning. Learning stimulates the mind. It is just like a muscle, in that if you don't use it, you might lose it.

Elizabeth Eichelbaum is a stellar example for all of us. At the age of 90, Elizabeth received her PhD in art therapy from the University of Tennessee. She received her bachelor's degree at 69, and her master's at age 81! During the final two years of her PhD., she attended classes in spite of macular degeneration (she's nearly blind). Her family says she is an inspiration to all who know her, and hope that it inspires others. It does.

If you have learned all you care to learn, what about teaching others? Teaching can be very mentally stimulating. There is always a need for volunteers at just about any endeavor, and could be just what you need to do.

"There is no exercise better for the heart than reaching down and lifting people up."

— John Andrew Holmes

If you knew this was your last day, what would be on your mind?

The other part of looking after mental balance involves the management of our thoughts. What's on your mind? Is it full of anger, jealousy, worry, bitterness, self pity, guilt? Is it what you would have on your mind, if you knew it was your last day? We can't control our thoughts, but we can certainly learn to manage them.

One of the things I had to learn to manage was my naturally competitive spirit. I've always been competitive. Growing up with a brother four and a half years older than me probably helped. So did my size. Being physically smaller than almost everyone helped develop my fighting spirit.

Then, at the age of 24, I entered one of the most massively competitive of all worlds — finance. Accustomed as I was to competition, it was like going from the frying pan into the fire. My thoughts became loaded with the desire to be Number One. I have no doubt my competitor spirit was instrumental in helping me get there.

But then something changed. I noticed that I no longer just *wanted* to be Number One, I *needed* to be Number One. There is a big difference.

Each month it was customary for the company to produce rating sheets. (Each of us are rated according to certain performance criteria.) If I looked at the monthly rating sheet and did not see my name right at the top as Number One, I was not a happy camper. Sometimes I became an unreasonably unhappy camper. Despite my efforts to pretend that it didn't matter, it did. It mattered a lot! My thoughts were *over*loaded with the desire to be first.

At that point, I decided it had gotten out of control, and I engaged a personal success coach.[1] I believe her sessions helped me get a new perspective on the meaning of being Number One. It was no longer the 'Be All and End All' of my life. I realized that, to me, the ultimate reward is watching my children grow up. And being with my wife.

I knew I'd won the war one day as I looked at a monthly rating sheet. That particular month I noticed I was *not* number one, and for the first time it was truly *okay*. I no longer rode the treadmill of competition. I still drove my clients' bottom lines as hard as ever, but my competitive spirit was tamed. I had altered of an out-of-balance need to be Number One.

Life is Short. Be Happy.

I've had two "wake up calls" in my adult life. The first occurred when my mother died. No one, except those who have experienced the loss of their mother, knows how painfully hard this can be. She was only 62 years old when she died, and it was sudden. It was hard for all of us in the family to come to grips with her death. My mother was very dearly loved.

A couple years later, while my family and I were in Palm Desert for spring break, I got my second wake up call.

[1] *Teresia LaRocque (Teresia@TLCSuccess.com)*

We were relaxing around the pool, and I was immersed in thoughts about my mother. I still felt the loss, and was learning that grieving is a process. I couldn't help thinking she was too young when she died. Ruthie had maintained a healthy lifestyle, never smoked cigarettes and rarely drank alcohol. I had always assumed she would live to a ripe old age. But she didn't, and I began to contemplate my own mortality. Out of the blue, I had an impulse to check in with my office in Vancouver, Canada.

"Life is too short," I remember thinking to myself as I went to make the phone call, strangely unable to ignore the impulse. There was no particular reason for me to call, but I felt compelled. It was a phone call I will remember for a long, long time.

As it turned out, there *was* news from the office. But it was not good news. It was shocking news, and the kind we all dread. I learned that a colleague had died. That morning. At his desk. Of a heart attack. He was only 42!

Ever since, I've had a little note stuck to my computer with the following words —

"Yesterday is history.
Tomorrow is a mystery.
Today is a gift."

I was profoundly affected by the realization of how short life is, and how it can all be over in a blink. I don't ever want to forget it. It makes me want to make the absolute best use of each and every day. I never want to take it for granted. I want to enjoy each day and appreciate everything about it. Each day is a precious gift.

I leave you with a poem that is dear to my heart. It expresses what I think is the most important lesson in life. It places both money and time on the grand scales of life.

Give Him a Day

What shall you give to one small boy?

A glamorous game, a tinseled toy?

A Boy Scout knife, a puzzle pack?

A train that runs on some curving track?

A picture book, a real live pet?

No, there's plenty of time for such things yet.

Give him a day of his very own.

A walk in the woods, a romp in the park.

A fishing trip from dawn to dark.

Give him the gift that only you can—

The companionship of his "Old Man."

Games are outgrown and toys decay,

But he'll never forget

If you give him a day.

—Author Unknown

Some people say that time is money. Nonsense. Money can be replaced. Time cannot. Time is the most precious thing we can spend. It is the most valuable of all gifts. Each day is a gift to cherish.

Each day, we have the opportunity to make the choices. We choose our attitude. We choose our actions. We choose our dreams. Each day we choose our future. Life happens one day at a time.

I hope this book has made a difference for you.

May your time with your loved ones be endless, and your life be full of P-O-W-E-R. And from this day forward, may you always be glad that...

tomorrow never lies.

—Ken Gordon, with Rachel Orr

Chapter 10 Review

- Without a purpose, life is empty.

- We need to know how much is enough.

- A man's character can be defined by what he is worth if he lost all his money.

- Once you've reached the top of that mountain you've been struggling to climb, find another mountain to climb.

- Life is a balancing act.

- The four elements to balance are: physical, emotional, spiritual and mental.

- Yesterday is history. Tomorrow is a mystery. Today is a gift.

"If you have grown wise and kind,
it is the measure of true success."

—Anonymous

Chapter Reviews

- There are no right or wrong dreams. Different people have different dreams.

- No one's dream is more important than ours.

- Living without a dream and a Life Plan is crazy.

- Our choices are inextricably linked with our attitudes.

- Each generation makes different choices and holds different attitudes.

- If you want to sell something to Boomers, tell them it will make them look younger, appear more attractive and successful, or offer instant gratification.

- The marketing tactics that work so well on Boomers fail miserably with younger generations.

- Boomers' choices and attitudes have made them woefully unprepared for their impending retirement.

- Younger generations are way ahead of Boomers when it comes to savings. They have different attitudes and make different choices.

Chapter 3

The Dangerous Money Myths are:

1. The equity in my home will be my retirement.

2. I will inherit my parents' money, so I don't have to worry.

3. There'll be safety in numbers.

4. I am so far behind in my investment plans that I must take excessive risks in order to catch up.

5. I'm looking forward to early retirement. I have nothing to worry about.

6. I've got plenty of time. I'm in no hurry to retire. I'll start my investment plan later.

7. There is nothing I can do. I've left it too long and now there is not enough time and/or there is not enough money left over at the end of the month to save.

Chapter 4

-   Attitude is a little thing that makes a big difference.

-   Faster has become synonymous with better. It isn't true.

-   We are in control of our attitude. Always.

-   Attitude is power. It levels the playing field.

- Our attitude determines our reaction. Our reaction creates the stress.

- Every decision, every choice has a price or a consequence.

- The first 5 minutes of every day sets our attitude.

- Self-talk can change an unproductive attitude.

- Beginning each day with a positive affirmation is extremely beneficial.

Chapter 5

- We say we don't have enough time, but the truth is that each of us has all the time there is.

- Successful people determine what is important to them, what they truly care about and then devote themselves to that pursuit.

- It is our responsibility to figure out our own priorities and what we value. Others' may be different than ours, and that's okay.

- We must put our big rocks (priorities) in the jar of life first.

- Our priorities should form the basis for our actions.

- Mismatched priorities will result in a lack or longing somewhere in our lives.

- We need to get clear about what we want and value, write it down and sign it.

Chapter 6 .... **121**

- The best financial plan ever is to stay married and have a good financial and Life Plan with our mate.

- Divorce costs. A lot. In lots of ways.

- Strong, long term relationships are built with "we" thinking and acting.

- If we can conceive it, and we believe it, we can achieve it

- Visualization works like magic if we practice it.

- Our children are always watching.

- It is time to begin getting my/our Binder together.

- We have the power to do and be whatever is within our capability.

- Without a plan, we are planning to fail.

- Life is an ongoing process. It is a journey, not a destination.

- We-thinking and acting help keep a marriage together.

- Having fun is important.

- It's good to reward ourselves when we reach our goals.

- There is a difference between investing and gambling. A big difference.

- The Investment Rules Are:

  a) Have a plan.

  b) Don't put all your eggs in one basket.

  c) Don't fiddle with your funds.

  d) The market will reward companies that make money.

- Everyone makes mistakes.

- Mistakes can be painful, but they can can also be wonderful opportunities.

- Our attitude effects our ability to deal with mistakes.

- How to Handle a Mistake:

  1. Admit it and accept it.

  2. Keep your eye on the ball.

  3. Learn from it, and forget about who to blame.

  4. Reach for each other.

  5. Be gentle with yourself.

  6. Control the damage.

  7 Focus on what is going right

  8. Never hesitate to seek help.

Chapter 9 .... **207**

- There is a world of difference between a good sound investment, and an investment that sounds good.

- The key to financial success lies in the ability to simplify the financial planning process, and obtain the guidance of a financial professional.

- Three things that can improve the relationship with a Financial Advisor are:

    1. Allow them to do their job, and take their advice.

    2. Be honest, and give the full picture.

    3. Understand that motion is not always progress.

- People who work with a financial advisor earn higher returns on their investment portfolios than those who try and do it on their own.

- Without a purpose, life is empty.

- We need to know how much is enough.

- A man's character can be defined by what he is worth if he lost all his money.

- Once you've reached the top of that mountain you've been struggling to climb, find another mountain to climb.

- Life is a balancing act of the 4 elements: physical, emotional, spiritual and mental.

- Yesterday is history. Tomorrow is a mystery. Today is a gift.